The SAMURAI

THE PHILOSOPHY OF VICTORY

ROBERT T. SAMUEL

BARNES
& NOBLE

NEW YORK

Language Consultant: Marion Duman, Carole Koplow
Layout and Graphics: Daniel Akerman

2005 Barnes & Noble Publishing

ISBN-13: 978-0-7607-7487-8
ISBN-10: 0-7607-7487-0

Printed and bound in China

5 7 9 10 8 6 4

Contents

Time

Period	Event	Year

Yamato Period

At the end of the 4th century, Japan was unified by the Yamato court.

Buddhism was introduced into Japan. ● 538

The Soga clan conquered the Mononobe clan. ● 587

Buddhism was proclaimed the official Japanese religion by regent Shotoku Taishi. ● 592

The Constitution in Seventeen Articles was introduced. ● 604

Asuka Period

Battle for imperial succession led to civil war. ● 672

The Code of Asuka no Kiyomihara was introduced. ● 689

Nara Period

The Japanese capital was established in Nara. ● 710

This is the official date of the history of Japan's origin. ● 720

From this time on, land that was newly cleared became private property. ● 743

A statue of the Great Buddha was constructed at Todai-ji. ● 749

The first poetry anthology, Manyoshu, was compiled. ● 790

Kyoto became the new Japanese capital. ● 794

Heian Period

Upon Saicho's return from Tang China, the Tendai sect was established. ● 805

Upon Kukai's return from Tang China, the Shingon sect was established. ● 816

Diplomatic missions to China were halted by Sugawara no Michizane. ● 894

The Hojo-ji temple, constructed by Fujiwara no Michinaga, was consecrated.
Fujiwara proclaimed the Fukiwara clan to be Japan's supreme leaders. ● 1022

Minamoto no Yoritomo mustered troops in Izu and invaded Kamakura. ● 1180

Kamakura Period

Minamoto no Yoritomo became shogun. ● 1192

The laws and principles of the Kamakura administration were drawn up in the *Joei shikimoku*. ● 1232

This was the year of the invasion by the Mongols. ● 1274

There was a further invasion by the Mongols. ● 1281

This year marked the end of the Kamakura administration. ● 1333

Northern and Southern dynasties split. ● 1336

Muromachi Period

Shogun Ashikaga Yoshimitsu defeated enemies and established the supremacy of his clan. ● 1368

Unification of Northern and Southern dynasties took place. ● 1392

Ashikaga Yoshimitsu abdicated, entered a monastic order, and had
the Golden Pavilion constructed. ● 1397

This was a year of peasant revolts. ● 1428

Civil war of succession to the shogunate began – this was a power struggle between the daimyos. ● 1467

Line

410	The Visigoths, led by Alaric, razed Rome. The Romans quit Britain.
420	This year marked the end of the Eastern Jin dynasty in China.
c.550	After attacks by the Huns, the Gupta empire in India ended.
c.570	Muhammed was born.
618	The Tang dynasty (618-907) was established in China. Order was restored by means of a strong centralizing power.
632	This year marked the peak of the Maya civilization.
634	Under Caliph Umar (634-44), Islam spread quickly in Arabia, Syria, Iran, and North Africa.
679	This year marked the decline of the Mexican Teotihuacán civilization.
732	Muslims were defeated at the Battle of Tours, which was led by the Merovingian "Mayor of Palace," Charles Martel.
768	Charlemagne, the king of the Franks (768-814) waged battles against the Avars and Saxons in the East.
794	Viking raids on England and Ireland took place. Jarrow and Iona were razed (795).
813	The Bulgars defeated Byzantine army at Adrianople. Constantinople was besieged by the Bulgars and the Arab army.
849	Burmans from Pagan unified Burma.
871	Alfred the Great became king of Wessex (871-899).
889	This year marked the end of the classic Old Mayan civilization in Mexico.
907	This year marked the end of the Tang dynasty in China, resulting in a fragmentation of the country.
935	The Koryo kingdom was established in Korea (935-1392). Its capital was Kaesong. The Buddhist religion flourished.
969	Western Arabia, Syria, and Egypt were conquered by the Fatimites. Cairo became their capital (973).
1035	Harold became king of England (1035-40).
1071	The Battle of Manzikert took place, in which the Seljuk Turks routed the Byzantine forces and threatened Asia Minor.
1077	At Canossa, Henry IV accepted papal supremacy to invest bishops.
1099	Crusaders captured Jerusalem.
1100	Henry I became king of England (1100-35).
1116	The Jin dynasty was established in Manchuria.
1165	William (the "Lion") became king of Scotland (1165-1214).
1168	Aztecs entered Mexico and destroyed the Toltec Empire.
1189	Richard I became king of England (1189-99).
1206	Genghis Kahn (1162-1227) proclaimed the Mongol empire.
1226	Louis IX became king of France (1226-70).
1250	The Mongol Mamelukes establised a dynasty in Egypt.
1261	Byzantines regained control of Constantinople.
1352	The Ottoman Turks entered Europe.

The Silver Pavilion was constructed for Ashikaga Yoshimitsu.	**1473**
Hojo Soun's seizure of Odawara castle marked the beginning of the period of the Warring Kingdoms.	**1495**
This year marked the arrival of the Portuguese at Kanegashima. It is a landmark in Japanese military history because this was when firearms were introduced into Japan.	**1543**
Spanish Jesuit Francis Xavier began his missionary endeavors.	**1549**
Ashikaga Yoshimitsu was deposed by Oda Nobunaga, marking the end of the Muromachi administration.	**1573**
Honoganji monks were subjected to supervision in accordance with Ashikaga Yoshimitsu's orders. The aim of this move was to curtail the military and secular power of the Buddhist monasteries.	**1580**
This year marked the assassination of Nobunaga and the accession of Toyotomi Hideyoshi.	**1582**
A castle was constructed by Hideyoshi in Osaka.	**1583**
Christianity was outlawed by Hideyoshi.	**1587**
Rural areas were banned from bearing arms. The privilege was reserved for nobles only.	**1588**
Hideyoshi reunified Japan.	**1590**
Monoyama castle was constructed by Hideyoshi.	**1594**
Hideyoshi died.	**1598**
The battle of Sekigahara resulted in Tokugawa Ieyasu seizing the power from the other daimyos.	**1600**
This was the period of Tokugawa Ieyasu's shogunate.	**1603**
Siege of Toyotomi castle in Osaka by Tokugawa Ieyasu took place.	**1615**
In Nagasaki, 55 Christians were killed.	**1622**
Foreigners were no longer permitted to enter Japan's ports.	**1636**
The Shimabar revolt took place when Christianity was banned in Japan.	**1637**
The Dutch established a settlement at Deshima.	**1641**
This was the year of the great fire of Edo.	**1657**
Restrictions pertaining to the parceling out of land were introduced.	**1673**
This was the year of great famine.	**1732**
This was another year of great famine.	**1783**
The ships of Commodore Perry weighed anchor in the bay of Edo.	**1853**
Trade with America was initiated when the Treaty of Kanagawa opened up the ports of Hakodate.	**1854**
Shimonoseki was bombarded by Western vessels.	**1864**
This year marked the end of the Tokugawa administration.	**1867**
The Meiji period began.	**1868**

Muromachi Period

Azuchi-Momoyama Period

Edo Period

The Hundred Years War was resumed, with the French commanded by Du Guesclin.

The Monal Tamerlane conquered Turkestan, Delhi, Persia, the Golden Horde, Syria, and Egypt (1363-1405).

The Ming dynasty was established by Shu Yuanshang (1368-1644) in China.

The infant Henry VI became king of England. The Council of Regency claimed France.

Uxmal conquered Mayan city of Mayapán.

Ottoman Turks conquered Constantinople.

Mongol Golden Horde was overthrown by Ivan III.

Columbus reached the West Indies.

Henry VIII became king of England (1509-47).

Mary Tudor became queen of England (1553-58) and persecuted the Protestants.

Akbar became emperor of India (1556-1605), expanding the empire and uniting its peoples.

The Turkish domination of the Mediterranean ended with the Battle of Lepanto.

Henry IV (1589-1610) accepted Catholicism in France.

This year marked the beginning of the Thirty Years War in Europe.

This year marked the beginning of the reign of the "Protector," Oliver Cromwell (1653-58).

Peter the Great became Tsar of Russar (1682-1725).

The Treaty of Nerchinsk was signed between China and Russia in order to determine borders.

This year marked the beginning of the reign of Queen Anne (1702-14).

Louis XV became king of France (1715-74).

George III became king of England (1760-1820).

Catherine the Great acceded to the throne, deposing her husband, Peter III, and becoming empress (1762-96)

Napoleon was born.

The "Boston Tea Party" took place, protesting against taxation without representation.

In America, the Declaration of Independence was signed on July 4 by 11 rebel colonies.

George Washington was elected the first president of the United States.

The French Revolution erupted. French aristocrats fled to England and Germany.

The War of 1812 took place between the United States and Britain (1812-14).

Victoria became queen of England (1837-1901).

This year marked the beginning of the first Opium War in China (1839-42).

This year marked the beginning of the Mexican-US War (1846-48).

This year marked the fall of the Second Republic in France.

The Battle of Gettysburg took place, yielding a Union victory.

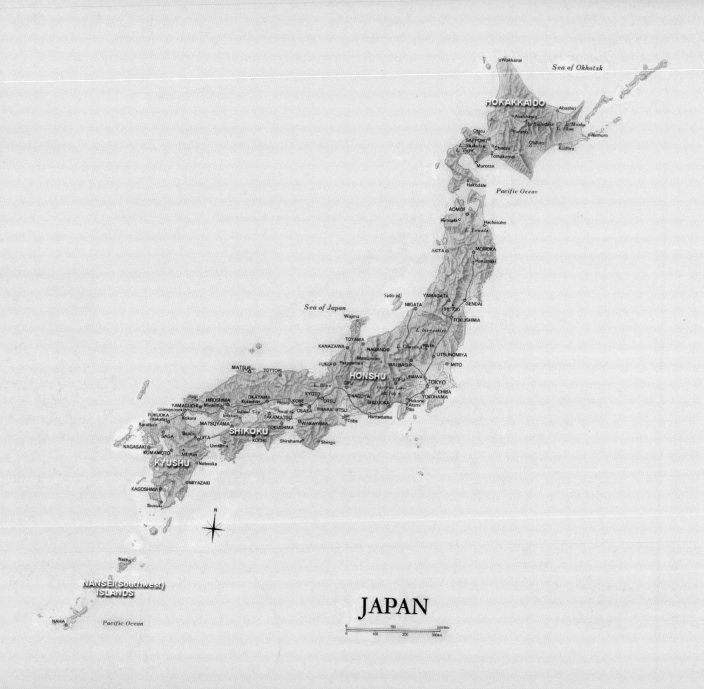

JAPAN

Sea of Okhotsk

oWakkanai

HOKAKKAIDO

Abashiri

oAsahikawa

Mt. Asahidake   L. Mashu
Otaru   oFurano   L. Akan

SAPPORO   Chitose   Obihiro   Nemuro
L. Shikotsu   Tomakomai   Kushiro
L. Toya

Muroran

Hakodate   *Pacific Ocean*

AOMOR

Hirosaki   Hachinohe

L. Towada

AKITA   MOROKA

Hanamaki

Sado isl.   YAMAGATA

Wajima   NIIGATA   SENDAI

Sea of Japan   Mt. Zao   FUKUSHIMA

TOYAMA   L. Inawashiro

KANAZAWA   NAGANO   L. Chuzenji

FUKUI   Matsumoto   UTSUNOMIYA

MATSUE   TOTTORI   Takayama   MAEBASHI   MITO

HONSHU   GIFU   KOFU   URAWA

L. Biwa   NAGOYA   TOKYO

Hagi   HIROSHIMA   KYOTO   OTSU   SHIZUOKA   CHIBA

YAMAGUCHI   OKAYAMA   Himeji   KOBE   Fuji Five Lakes   YOKOHAMA

Shimonoseki   Kurashiki   Awaji isl. OSAKA   Mt. Fuji   Hakone

FUKUOKA   Imabari   *Island Sea*   NARA   TSU   Atami

(Hakata)   Kokura   MATSUYAMA   TAKAMATSU   Hamamatsu

Karatsu   TOKUSHIMA   Toba

SAGA   Beppu   **SHIKOKU**   WAKAYAMA

NAGASAKI   Uwajima   KOCHI   Shirahama   Shingu

KUMAMOTO   OITA

KYUSHU   Mt. Aso

Nobeoka

KAGOSHIMA   MIYAZAKI

Ibusuki

N

Naze

**NANSEI (Southwest)
ISLANDS**

NAHA   *Pacific Ocean*

100   200 Mile

100   200   300km

Bushi

"**B**USHI" should actually be the correct name of this book, central to which is the Japanese warrior, and the Japanese art of military combat during over a millennium and a half.

The title "Bushi" was assigned to warriors born to established military clans – families of considerable substance and means, with a known fighting tradition. The family would equip and support the warrior, while he underwent training and exercises, as the military dictated.

The Bushi were ranked according to a scale which took into account the family's standing, the fighter's ability, and his military accomplishments. Rank also pertained to the Bushi's relation to the Shogun, the highest Bushi. The Samurai were simply Bushi of a higher class and rank.

The Bushi warriors began to appear in Japan during the 7th century. The first Bushi were farmers and fishermen who divided their time between agricultural occupations and military training and active duty. Beginning in the 9th century, Bushi who excelled as fighters began to serve as full time paid warriors.

Over the years, the Bushi families evolved into dynasties. Rights, responsibilities, and duties would be passed from the fathers to the sons.

When a warrior family's status became established, youngsters of the clan were educated for fighting from childhood. They were tutored in horseback riding, archery, and fencing. Other studies included calligraphy, ethics, mathematics, Japanese history, and selected "Bushido" literature.

During the period that the Bushi solidified their stand as a group, the Samurai, who were high ranking Bushi, began to stand out. The Samurai were loyal servants of their lords. In time the term Samurai came to mean a fighter under obligation to serve his master. Later, Samurai virtually took over the term Bushi, in Japan as well as in the West.

However the Bushi did not disappear. The Tao of the Warrior, or The Way of the Warrior, is known until today as the Bushido (and not as the Samuraido!). Also, when Japanese military is discussed in wider terms, Bushi is the word used. For example, women warriors are termed Bushi Women, and not Samurai Women.

We will discuss the principles of the Bushido in a later chapter.

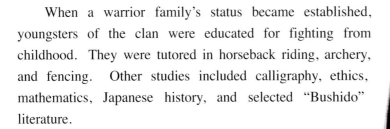

As mentioned, Samurai was actually one rank along the Bushi class scale. At first, it delineated the warriors who defended and fought alongside the feudal lords, or other members of an imperial court. Later, it became synonymous with any fighter who achieved a certain rank and above.

In the 12th century, the lords received the title Daimyo, or Feudal Baron, and one of the Daimyo received the title Shogun, the highest ranked Bushi.

Some important concepts to keep in mind when reading this book:

BUSHI – Warrior born into a clan with an honorable military tradition.

SHOGUN – Rich and powerful lord - above him was only the Emperor (which is not a military rank).

DAIMYO - Feudal lord - the Samurai would swear allegiance to him.

SAMURAI – Particular class of warrior family which defended the Daimyos. Warriors highly trained in the military arts. Over time Samurai became synonymous with Bushi (warriors).

RONIN – Bushi or Samurai who were under no obligation or loyalty to a particular lord, or a Samurai whose lord was deceased, or whose lord had been banished and his property confiscated. Actually, the Ronin functioned as "hired swords" and their very existence went to a certain extent against the stance and principles of the Samurai. The title Ronin took the place of the term Nobushi, or Bushi who hired out his services and was not obligated to any lord.

NINJA – Warriors of a low rank. Not from families of established warrior status. The Ninja served various lords – usually as Guerilla fighters, assassins, or spies.

Bushi Women

The Japanese wars dragged on for many hundreds of years. Thus the hardships and dangers of war were experienced by each and every household. The warriors, the Samurai, and the fighters they commanded, would form groups and set out to fight the enemy, leaving behind homes and families with no defense, or protected only by servants of the lowest ranking Bushi class. During the difficult period of the 15th and 16th centuries, a feudal lord made this entry in his diary: "Today the last fit man left his home and went out to be conscripted as a Nobushi to whomever would hire his services; and he being lame, lacking archery, sword, or javelin skills."

In fact, the Samurai left at home only women, young children, and the frail elderly. War took the Samurai quite a distance from home, leaving its defense in the hands of the women.

It must be remembered that an attack on the home or family of an enemy was common among the warriors. Any vulnerability of the enemy could be taken advantage of. In addition, since the Samurai warrior was based in a clan of tradition and standing in warfare, destruction of his family would cut the roots of the Samurai and prevent revenge by future offspring of that family.

We find numerous descriptions of women who learned to handle weapons and to defend themselves and their kin. Some women carried into battle a weapon called a "naginata", which was a long spear, swung like a scythe from side to side.

But the more common weapon carried by women was the well known dagger called the "kaiken". Every woman of Samurai status carried a kaiken, and was trained in its use. Were a woman to be attacked within reach of her kaiken, she would not hesitate to use it to defend her honor. In battle, a woman would hold the dagger with two hands, with the blade toward the face, and charge the enemy in order to deliver a fatal blow.

The woman's dagger was used mainly to carry out suicide ceremonies, called Jigai. Suicide such as this was parallel to the Seppuku (abdomen slicing) of the Samurai, but it entailed instead the slitting of the throat.

We must remember that women who were beaten or defeated in battle were expected to be raped, to become servants, or to be murdered. A woman's honor was paramount to her and to her family, and disgrace was seen as a fate worse even than death. The female warrior saw in the battle with no hope (which was essentially suicide) a way to be rescued from such shame. Thus often they would fight "to the death", or escape disgrace through performing the Jigai ceremony.

There were instances also of women fighters who alone or at the head of a group of fighters, managed to beat the enemy!

Death is a central aspect

Death is a central aspect of the Way of the Samurai. When a samurai is faced with a situation in which he has to choose between life and death, his immediate, unhesitating choice is death. He must be resolute and not preoccupy himself with the thought that dying without realizing one's ambitions is an ignoble death. This is a glib excuse. Realizing one's ambitions is secondary when one is faced with the choice of living or dying.

While the desire to live is natural, and we temper our actions according to this desire, there is no doubt that opting for life without realizing our ambitions is cowardly. Even though dying without realizing one's ambitions is indeed an ignoble death, and that of a zealot, there is nothing reprehensible about it. This epitomizes the Way of the Samurai. A successful samurai should put his heart in order first thing in the morning and last thing at night. In this way, his life is immaculate, since he lives as if his body is no longer alive. He strides unencumbered along the Way.

Hagakura - Yamamoto Tsunetomo

Hojo Soun's 21 Articles

1 Believe in Buddha and the Shinto gods.

2 Get up early in the morning in order to set a good example for your servants and to carry out your own duties well. If you begin to be lax, you'll be fired.

3 Go to bed at a reasonable hour. Don't waste fuel for lighting while you hang out with other guys until late at night. Remember that robbers usually break in two hours before and after midnight, so if you aren't around, you'll fall victim to them. It's not worth getting a bad name for irresponsible behavior. Get up a couple of hours before dawn, wash in cold water, and say your prayers. Get yourself ready, and then give your wife, children and servants their instructions for the day. Arrive at work early, before the sun rises, so that you can do all the work allotted to you. If you don't keep up, you won't be able to do everything you're responsible for.

4 Before washing your face and hands, go and check out the washroom, the gates, stables, and gardens. Get someone to clean up the places that need cleaning. Then go and wash your face and hands. Don't expectorate loudly, because this will disturb the people asleep in your house.

5 Saying prayers is for your own sake. Be honest, sincere, and law-abiding. Respect your superiors and treat your subordinates compassionately. Accept your lot, in accordance with Buddha and the Shinto gods: accept what you have and what you don't have – this will give you divine protection, even if you don't pray. Remember if a dishonest person prays, he will not be given divine protection. Beware!

6 Don't try and compete with others in the quality of your clothes and weapons. As long as they look reasonable, you're fine. If you go into debt to buy expensive things, people will deride you.

7 Fix your hair first thing, whether you go to work or stay at home. There is no way you can appear among people when you're all disheveled – and if your servants see that you don't care about your appearance, they'll begin to neglect theirs, too. It also looks ridiculous for you to rush to fix your hair if an unexpected guest arrives.

8 When you arrive at work, don't go straight to the boss's office. Wait in the waiting area and see how the other workers behave. Go to the boss when he calls you, otherwise there may be an unpleasant surprise in store for you.

9 When the boss calls you, answer "Yes, sir!" promptly, even if you are at some distance from him. Hurry forward, and then, when you get close to him, crawl to him on your hands and knees. Then rush off to do what he has told you to do, and when you're done, come back and give him an accurate report. Don't try and show how clever you are. If necessary, consult with other people as to how to present your report to the boss. Don't take all the credit.

10 When you are with your boss, don't listen to gossips. Keep well away from them. You must also not talk about yourself or laugh loudly – this will make your cronies and your boss ostracize you.

11 Rely on others – don't try to do things alone.

12 Carry a book with you wherever you go, so that if you have a free moment, you can read and revise the characters surreptitiously. If you don't get into the habit of reviewing them, you'll forget them. Do the same for writing.

13 When there is a line of VIPs waiting to consult with your boss, do not walk past them arrogantly, but bow at the waist and hold your hands low. Samurai must behave with humility and deference.

14 Always tell the truth to everyone – whether they are superior or subordinate to you. Even when you are joking, tell the truth, otherwise telling half-truths and lies will become a habit and you will be ostracized. If someone accuses you of lying, it is a disgrace that will never leave you.

15 If you don't know tanka composition, you are ignorant and ungifted. You must study it. Always watch what you say. One word can betray your thoughts.

16 During your free time, practice your equestrian skills. Get an expert to show you the basic stuff, and learn all the rest on your own.

17 Spend your time on studying and writing. Avoid go, chess, and musical instruments. It's not that there's anything wrong with these things – they're just a waste of time. Remember that the type of person you are – good or bad – depends on your friends. Remember, too, that when you are traveling with two other people, one of them will be worth listening to. Choose him. The other one can serve as an example of what not to do.

18 When you're off work and go home, check out certain things, such as whether the walls of your house, behind the stables, are intact. Repair the holes in the fence made by dogs. If the thatch from the roof has been used for heating, replace it.

19 At sunset, lock the gate. Open it only if someone comes or goes. This will prevent trouble.

20 Before going to sleep, check out all the fires in the kitchen and your wife's room, as well as ensuring that your house can't be harmed by a neighbor's fire. Do this every night, since wives tend to forget this, and leave their clothes and jewelry lying around. If you have servants, you must first do things yourself before you ask them to do them. It is important for you to know what it's like to do things.

21 It is imperative for you to constantly practice reading, writing, martial arts, archery, and equestrian skills. Literary skills belong to your left hand, martial skills to your right.

Hojo Soun, 1490

A man who was killed in a fight

Failing to perform some administrative duty can be attributed to ineptitude and a lack of experience. However, when men demonstrate cowardice instead of performing what is expected of them, they should commit seppuku rather than live with the ignominy of their situation and the resulting ostracism and bad name. If a person feels that his death would be a waste and that he should live longer, he will be a despised outcast. When he dies, his corpse will be shrouded in disgrace, and everyone connected to him – innocent descendants, forebears, and family, will be tainted with his shame.

A warrior who does not live with resolve, whose whole being is not involved in being a warrior, or who spends his days in idleness, deserves to be punished.

A man who was killed in a fight can be said to have run out of luck. His killer, who had no choice but to kill him, cannot be considered a coward. The two adversaries were not cowards. However, if men choose to live rather than face death, they are not true warriors, and deserve nothing but ignominy.

It is important to engrave the saying, "There is no time like the present," into one's mind, and not procrastinate or act negligently. The Way of the Samurai is a study of death – where, when and how it should happen, and getting oneself into the state of mind for receiving it. Hard as this may be to do, where there's a will, there's a way, and one should not have a defeatist attitude.

In military matters, words have a great effect as well. If a man is trying to flee, shouting to him that only cowards run could have the desired effect of stopping him and letting him fight it out instead of escaping. It is no good putting things off, and one should resolve to follow this way of acting.

There are many things that must be considered carefully before acting. A person who has killed a man in a lord's palace and may still be on his way to killing the lord must be apprehended, since his intentions are unclear. Even though the person who killed him may afterwards face some blame, such as being in collaboration with the assassin or bearing some kind of grudge against him, the person should act now and think later, and not hesitate because he is thinking of possible consequences.

Hagakura

Military Service

Combat and construction are the official duties of warriors. During wartime, the warrior is constantly in action, and cannot let up for a moment. Construction is an integral part of warfare: a bridge has to be built, a ditch dug, a fortress or outpost erected – usually post-haste, entailing the strenuous toil of warriors, from the lowest to the highest in rank.

During peacetime, the warriors are obliged to perform miscellaneous duties and errands. These can include service as guards, couriers, escorts, and more. Anyone who thinks that this is basically what warriors do is completely mistaken. The warriors are required to share the expenses for public projects commissioned by the shogun. If anyone thinks that this is unjust, he is unaware that combat and construction are the essential duties of the warrior.

If a warrior fakes illness in order to shirk the peacetime duties mentioned above and he has no compunction about landing his comrades with the job, he is not a true warrior. He is like a lowly servant disguised as a knight. He may moan and complain about having to carry out these errands or duties, and his bad attitude will reflect negatively on him. The reason for his reluctance may stem from the fact that he does not want to travel in inclement weather conditions, pay for his travel expenses, or confront the difficulties on the road. There is no excuse for his behavior: this is what his profession demands.

He should bear in mind the hardships of the warriors who served during the Era of the Warring States: during that time, the warriors suffered from extreme heat in summer, bitter cold in winter, sleeping fully armed in the open, regardless of weather conditions, and eating the worst food. Their lives consisted of battle and hard labor. If a warrior thinks of what the alternative could be, he should be very grateful that he can lead a normal life, with all its creature comforts – even if he has to do an occasional stint of guard duty or serve as an escort or courier once in a while. A famous warrior adopted the slogan: "Always on the Battlefield." Warriors, take note!

The first thing one has to do in the morning

When Lord Mitsushige was a young child, the priest, Kaion, asked him to recite from a text. Before doing so, the child called the other children and priests to listen to his recitation. According to him, it was hard to read when hardly anybody was present. Kaion admired the child for this, and told his followers that this was the way everything should be done.

The first thing one has to do in the morning is to pay homage to one's master and parents, and only afterwards to the patron gods and guardian Buddhas. It is important for a man to honor his master first. His parents will be pleased about it, and the gods and Buddhas will agree to his action. It is essential for a warrior to think about his master only, because this will make the warrior constantly aware of his master, and he will never abandon him – even for the shortest time.

Just as a warrior thinks about his master first, so it is incumbent upon a woman to think of her husband first.

Hagakura

Equestrian skills

Archery and equestrian skills were once considered to be the elite of the martial arts. Nowadays, swordsmanship, lancing, and equestrian skills are the arts that warriors focus on. Other martial arts such as jujitsu, archery, and so on, should be learned and practiced when the warrior is young and it is easier to acquire them.

Even warriors who are not top-class should learn to ride well so that they are not fazed by any horse, however mean and undisciplined it may be. This also enables the warrior to purchase a good horse with a less than ideal temperament for a low price. In this way, he has a better horse than he could ordinarily afford. Another aspect of purchasing a horse is color and the quality of its coat. These things should not enter the considerations of a less than top-class warrior. The only thing he should worry about is how good the horse is.

An example of the above is the warrior called Kakuganji, who commanded 300 horsemen for the Murakami clan. He was in the habit of purchasing agile horses that did not have good coats. Leading groups of 50 or 100 horsemen over the plains near the castle, he would have them execute flying mounts and dismounts, thereby turning them into expert equestrians. They were so skilled that even the fearsome Takeda clan thought several times before challenging Kakuganji's mounted troops.

Traditionally, a warhorse should be of average height, and his head and hindquarters should be of average size. However, for a lower-rank warrior who owns only one horse, the horse should have a large body, stand tall, and have broad hindquarters – even though broad hindquarters are not considered to be suitable for narrow paths.

It is a reprehensible custom to stretch the horse's leg sinews in order to increase the length of its strides (because it will quickly become tired on an incline, on a long journey, or during a river crossing), or to cut the tail sinew so that it is unable to lift its tail (because it will slip its crupper when crossing a riverbed or a canal, thus dislodging the saddle).

The ancient warriors, who were heavily armed, used horses as a substitute for their own feet. They were concerned for their horses' welfare and safety, and fed and curried them after riding them. Nowadays, however, the aim of buying recalcitrant horses or country-bred colts at bargain prices is to train them and sell them to the highest bidder. The interest of the brokers is solely mercenary; the actual horses are of no consequence at all.

The Bakufu

Yorimoto established his rule in Kamakura, far from the temptations of Kyoto. He was loyal to the emperor, but considered himself to be the true wielder of power in Japan. When the emperor died in 1192, and his teenage grandson, Go-Toba, succeeded him, Yorimoto exploited the situation to reinforce his power as much as possible. He convinced Go-Toba not only to appoint him shogun but also to make the position hereditary. Now he was a fully-fledged military dictator.

The Kamakura government required not only military talent, but administrative skills as well. Many scholars were employed at the Bakufu, and they set up a three-part administrative system: (1) The samurai-dokoro, which, as its name suggests, concerned the samurai. It was a court that dealt with matters of honor, conduct, promotions, military strategy, and samurai ethics. (2) The man-dokoro, which handled the everyday administration of the Bakufu – a kind of civil service, headed by Oe Hiromoto. (3) The moncho-jo, a court of appeals that dealt with property disputes that could not be settled at a lower level. This prevented a lot of unnecessary property-based warfare.

However, a leopard does not change its spots. Just as Yorimoto had been instrumental in Yoshitsune's death, so he had many potential "threats" removed from among his family, the first of them being his half-brother Noriyori in 1193. Six years later, when Yorimoto was killed in a riding accident, there was no one left in his family to succeed him. According to legend, Yoshitsune's ghost spooked Yorimoto's horse, which promptly threw him – thus giving Yoshitsune his revenge for his brother's ill-treatment.

The First Shoguns

Shogun Otomo Yakamochi was appointed in 784 with the express purpose of defeating the Ainu and their allies. He failed dismally in this task, and died two years later – his major claim to fame being the fact that he initiated a millennium of shogun rule. His successor, Ki no Kosami, was also ordered to wipe out the Ainu. To this end, he was assigned 52,000 cavalry and infantry troops. However, his losses in a single battle were so outrageous and ignominious (soldiers being thrown into the river with or without their armor and drowning, for instance) that the emperor, Kammu, incensed with rage, had Kosami and his generals tried and sentenced to death. Their sentences were commuted, however. The reason for their total failure against the enemy was the policy of appointment according to the "old boy" system of patronage rather than according to merit and achievement.

In 790, in an attempt to tackle the Ainu problem more vigorously, a tax was levied on the population of all the provinces, including nobles and officials. In this way, tons of rice and other foods were collected, and close to 40,000 suits of leather and metal armor were requisitioned. Close to 350,000 arrows were manufactured. A survey was conducted in order to catch all draft-dodgers and tax-evaders and compel them to contribute additional supplies to the war effort.

These operations took several years, and it was not until 794 that the next shogun, Otomo Otomaro, a noble from the family that guarded the emperor, was appointed.

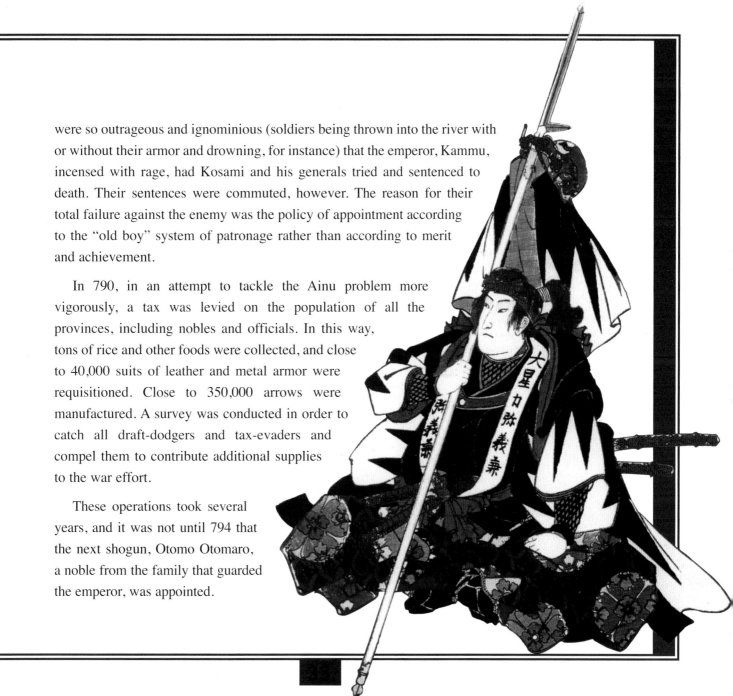

In order to progress in life

An aging swordsman spoke about the stages in the pursuit of knowledge. During the first stage, studies lead to nothing, and the person thinks that he and other people lack skills. He is worth nothing. During the middle stage, he is still worth nothing, but is now aware of his worthlessness and can see it in others. During the next stage, he prides himself on his achievements and is praised for them, but abhors other people's inadequacy. He is worthy. At the highest stage, the person looks as if he knows nothing.

However, there is one more stage – the supreme one. The person realizes that the Way is endless and that he will never complete it. He is aware of his shortcomings and denies any successes. He is humble, but recognizes the full length of the Way. He applies his knowledge to himself, and no longer to others.

In order to progress in life, one has to improve every day in an endless process.

Hagakura

General Yogo's Head

In the province of Mutsu, there was an ongoing feud between two warriors, Taira no Koremochi, nicknamed "Yogo," and Sawamata no Shiro, based on the ownership of some insignificant agricultural land. The situation deteriorated further as a result of malicious gossip that maligned both parties.

Finally, neither side being able to tolerate any more slander, they decided to confront each other with their soldiers and let the best man win. Yogo's forces numbered about 3,000, but Sawamata could muster no more than 1,000. Realizing that he didn't stand a chance against Yogo's superior numbers, Sawamata canceled the confrontation and quit Mutsu. Yogo was suspicious of this move, and remained on the alert with his forces for a few days. However, after hearing rumors that Sawamata had been seen strutting around the neighboring province of Hitachi, Yogo decided to let his men go.

Some time later, Yogo was awakened in the middle of the night by the screeching of the birds in the pond near his house. He realized that he was about to be attacked, and he ordered the small number of soldiers who were on the premises to prepare for battle. The scout he sent returned to say that there seemed to be a large number enemy of soldiers nearby. Realizing that the odds were against him, Yogo decided to fight to the death. He sent his wife, infant, and some of the maids to a safe place behind the house, and then the fighting began. Sawamata set fire to the house, and anyone trying to escape was mowed down on the spot. The death toll in the fire reached about 80 people – men and children – and some of the corpses were so blackened that it was impossible to identify them. Sawamata was pretty sure that Yogo was among the dead – after all, no one could escape either the conflagration or instant death outside the house – so he began his retreat, carrying his own wounded on horseback.

He decided to stop for food and rest at the home of his brother-in-law, the Great Prince. The latter praised the brilliant strategy that had enabled Sawamata to kill the cunning Yogo, and requested to see Yogo's head, which should have been attached to Sawamata's saddle. Of course, Sawamata didn't have the head, so he scoffed at the Prince's request, saying that there was no way that Yogo could have escaped. The Prince was not convinced, and since he had not been shown incontrovertible evidence of Yogo's grisly death, he didn't want Sawamata and his forces on his premises, just in case Yogo was in fact still around and would later attack him for having been hospitable to Sawamata.

Sawamata had no choice but to take his men and leave the Great Prince's estate. They found a hill and a stream fairly nearby, and decided to rest there. As they were removing their

weapons and letting their horses graze, the Great Prince's servants arrived with a veritable feast for the soldiers, and food for the horses. The effect of a few glasses of sake on an empty stomach was lethal, and it didn't take long for every last man and horse to sprawl out exhausted (and blind drunk, in the case of the soldiers) on the ground.

Meanwhile, Yogo, far from being a corpse, had escaped the slaughter by dressing up as a lowly maid, wading into the stream, and laying low until Sawamata and his men had left. Suddenly, about 40 of his original forces, who had heard of the fiery battle, raced up on horseback, weeping when they realized that Yogo had perished. They were overjoyed when Yogo suddenly announced his presence. After they had re-equipped themselves, Yogo explained in order to justify his rather cowardly escape from the burning house, where so many of his own people had met their deaths, he would go and attack Sawamata alone. This would expunge the shame of his actions for future generations. He was not prepared to risk the lives of more of his men. The latter suggested that he wait until he could muster a large army, and then attack Sawamata, but he was adamant.

He set off alone on a huge stallion, but his men – altogether about 100 – followed him immediately. He reckoned that it was imperative to strike on that particular day, because Sawamata and his forces would no doubt be dead to the world from exhaustion and food, and this would be the perfect opportunity to defeat them, even if his forces were vastly inferior in number to Sawamata's.

As they passed the Great Prince's house, Yogo sent a message to say that he was still alive.

Yogo and his men soon discovered where Sawamata was camped. Immediately he launched his attack. The enemy troops, who were barely conscious, were thrown into total confusion, and attempted to arm themselves, saddle their horses, or flee. A massacre ensued, during which Sawamata was beheaded.

Yogo returned to Sawamata's house with his soldiers. The occupants mistakenly thought that this was the triumphant return of Sawamata, but too late they realized their error. Yogo set fire to the house and killed anyone who tried to escape. However, he took Sawamata's wife and maid aside, had them dress up in lowly clothes, and instructed his soldiers to set fire to the entire compound, to kill any man they saw, but not to touch any woman.

After Yogo was satisfied that his instructions had been carried out, he took Sawamata's wife to her brother, the Great Prince, and left a message that she had not been mistreated. He then set out on his return journey to what remained of his own estate. His reputation as a supreme warrior was firmly established.

The art of bearing the armor

Have any of you ever timed how long it takes for a teenager to decide what to wear? Every time I'm to leave the house with my wife and teenage children, I spend a long hour in my favorite armchair watching the last stages of the ceremony of getting dressed. Yet, I always console myself with the thought that if I were married to, or a father of, a Samurai, this whole ceremony of getting dressed would take much, much longer!

The official dress of the Samurai was expensive, intricately detailed, and very formal. The best description of the Samurai wardrobe is found in books describing "the art of bearing the armor", such as Hi Ko Ben from the 18th century. We present the 18 stages or layers of the dress and armor of the Samurai of the 15-17 centuries, from these sources.

It is important to remember – and this is why we give a detailed description of the dress of the Samurai – that the strict ritual of the warrior's dress (Busi) is part of the Bushido tradition that also included detailed rules of everyday activities, for example the cleaning of the warrior's sword, drinking tea, writing letters.

And now, with great patience, let us dress the naked Samurai for battle.

Fundoshi (loincloth)

This item of clothing is made out of white linen or white cotton, although silk crepe (not plain silk) can also be used. In winter, it may be lined with similar material, but it is otherwise worn as a single layer. The front and back have cords running through them so that the front is anchored by looping around the neck, while the back one is secured by being tied at the front.

Shitagi (shirt)

The shitagi is a plain garment reminiscent of the kimono, but is shorter, narrower and with narrow sleeves. It has buttons on the breast and a wide cord around the waist. First, the left arm and then the right arm are put through the sleeves, the breast is buttoned, and the cord is tied at the back.

Kobakama (breeches)

There are various styles of kobakama, but they all end about 10 cm below the knees. To wear them, first put the left leg and then the right leg into the breeches. Then tie the back cords in the front, and the front cords in the front as well.

履職子
穿脚絆

Kiahan (gaiters)

These are made from either cotton or, preferably, linen. The inner cords are shorter than the outer ones, and they should be tied and knotted on the inner leg otherwise the knots will cause discomfort when the shinguards are put on over them.

Waraji (sandals)

Waraji are made from durable material such as hemp, ginger stalks, palm fibers, rice straw. The cords which tie the waraji to the feet can be tied in various ways, but it is important to tie an extra tie across the instep in order to make marching over various terrain easier. Six tabs on the sandals prevent stones from getting in the sandals. An extra pair of sandals must be carried at the waist.

筑草鞋

着脛當

Suneate (shinguards)

The most popular type of suneate was made from vertical plates joined together by hinges or chainmail, and were often lined with material. A leather guard is attached to the inner side of the area that comes into contact with the stirrups. The left guard is put on first with the part called abumi-zure on the inner leg. Then the cords are tightly tied.

Haidate (thighguards)

This is an apron-like cloth with either overlapping plates of metal or leather on the lower section, and a cord at the waist. After putting on the rest of the leg and foot gear, the center of the upper border of the haidate is placed at the front of the torso, and the cords are wrapped around the waist and tied in front over the haidate. They are worn under the do, but tied over it to allow for free movement and fast removal.

Yugake (gloves)

These are made of tanned skin and are usually unlined. When putting on the gloves, put the right one on first. This departure from the rule (of the left first) is because the right hand has more ability than the left one, and can tie the cords on the left one (while gloved) more easily.

Kote (sleeves)

The kote are varied but the sleeves are usually made from silk brocade, which is padded and has cords on the inner arm. It is covered with small metal plates or quilting with metal plates sewn in. Metal plates to protect the hand are attached to the kote, and these cords must only be tied at the end as they limit movement. The right kote is removed when shooting.

Do (body armor) and kusazuri (skirts)

This piece includes the back and breast plates as well as the laminated skirt. There are many types of armor. To put it on, the warrior sits in the shown position, holds the do toward himself and opens the sides. He takes the flap in his right hand and puts the do on his knee. He inserts his left arm into the do and pulls it to cover his body. He folds the front flap onto the back one and ties the upper cords in a "flower knot". He ties the cords on the left of the waist, putting one at the back and one at the front. The back cord is passed through a ring at the side of the body and is tied in the front.

Uwa obi (belt)

This is made from linen or cotton cloths wound 2-3 times around the body. The cloth is folded into half and twisted. Then a piece of leather is inserted in the center (so that the middle is easy to find in the dark). Put this mark against the front of the do and use the "flower knot" to tie the two ends in front after winding them around the back.

Wakibiki (armpit protectors)

The tsunagi wakibiki (where the two sides are connected so the garment is one piece) must be worn by putting the arms through the shoulder loops and then fastening the cords at the chest.

Sode (shoulder guards)

Fasten the left and then the right guard to the do by the hooks. First do the back and then the front. The more important the officer, the bigger the shoulder guards.

Katana (long sword) and tanto (dagger)

The tanto is single-edged and has a wrought iron guard and a short handle, which is as long as the width of a hand. The dagger is put between the belt and the cords tying the do, and is tied there by twisting the silk cord around the scabbard of the dagger.

Nodowa (throat protector)

There are many types of throat armor, of which the nodowa is one. The nodowa also has many shapes and styles and is fastened at the nape of the neck with cords.

Hachimaki (head cloth)

This is wrapped around the head to pad it before putting on the helmet. It is made from either light blue or reddish-yellow cotton. First, the warrior brushes his hair back and then places the center of the cloth behind his head. He then winds it round his head and tucks the ends into the folds.

Hoate (face mask)

There are a variety of mask which cover different areas of the face. The mask with a nosepiece is called menpo and there are 6 styles which all cover the cheeks and chin. A moveable nosepiece and a mustache are recommended. A handkerchief is put between the mask and chin, and the cords are tied on the top of the head, slightly to the back.

Kabuto (helmet)

There are many different styles of helmet and suspended neck guard (sides and back). The helmet is put on from behind and is pulled forward. Then the front loop of the cord is put under the chin, and the ends of the main cord are thread through metal rings in the helmet. These cords are pulled upward, passed through other cords in the helmet, and pulled down to be tied under the chin. The tied ends are twisted and tucked under the cheeks of the mask.

*D*enko, a priest, had a mother, an older brother, Jirobei, and a younger brother. One day, Denko's mother took her grandson, Jirobei's son, to the temple, and on the way out, when the child was putting on his sandals, he accidentally trod on another man's foot. The man became furious, the two argued violently, and the man killed both the child and the flabbergasted grandmother. His name was Gorouemon, son of Moan, and brother of the ascetic, Chuzobo. Moan was Master Mimasaka's advisor.

Upon hearing of the incident, Denko's younger brother went to Gorouemon's home and, when the door was opened, announced who he was, killed Gorouemon, and was then killed by Chuzobo. Denko wanted Jirobei to go and kill Chuzobo in order to try and equalize the number of casualties in his family, but Jirobei would not agree to do so.

Denko was disgusted with him, and decided that, although he himself was a priest, he would have to avenge his family's deaths. As an ordinary priest, however, he would not have any protection from Mimasaka's reprisals. So he studied hard for a year and became a chief priest, and then had a long and a short sword made.

About a year after the killings, he slipped out of his priest's dwelling in disguise, and went off in search of Chuzobo, who was busy watching the moon with a crowd of people. Not willing to postpone the deed any more, Denko decided that the father, Moan, would be just as good a target, so he broke into Moan's house and killed him. Even though the neighbors surrounded him, he explained the situation, discarded his weapons, and went home, where he was greeted by his congregants.

Because of Denko's high status, the irate Mimasaka was unable to do anything. However, he saw to it that another of the chief priests punished Denko by defrocking and banishing him, in accordance with the Buddhist law pertaining to renegade priests.

After his robes were confiscated, Denko was escorted out by some novices and a crowd of congregants, who accompanied him for a long way. He moved to another province, where he was welcomed – by samurai as well. There he was well treated for the rest of his life.

Hagakura

The History of the Taia Sword

Apparently, as a master of martial arts I do not fight in order to win or lose, I do not think of strength or weakness and I do not advance a step or retreat a step, the enemy does not see me. I do not see the enemy. When I penetrate a place in which heaven and earth have not yet separated, where Yin and Yang have not yet been created, I necessarily gain an effect rapidly.

Apparently indicates something that I do not know for certain.

In the original, the meaning of the character that indicates this word was "cover." For instance, when the sky covers a row of boxes, then although they do not know for certain what was placed in them, if we use our imagination we will hit the bull's-eye six or seven times out of ten. Here too I do not know for sure, but rather tentatively figure that that is how it should be. In fact, we use the word "apparently" even for things that we do actually know for certain. We do this in order to be modest and not to appear as if we are speaking in a knowing manner.

A master of martial arts is an expression that is self-evident in meaning.

Not to fight in order to win or lose, not to think of strength or weakness, means not to compete with the aim of winning or worry about defeat, and not to think about strength or weakness.

Not to advance a step or retreat a step means not to take one step forward or one step backward. Victory is achieved without budging from your place.

The word "me" in the expression, "the enemy does not see me," relates to **my true self.** It does not refer to the perceived self.

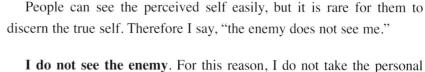

People can see the perceived self easily, but it is rare for them to discern the true self. Therefore I say, "the enemy does not see me."

I do not see the enemy. For this reason, I do not take the personal view[1] of the visible self, I do not see the martial art of the perceived self of the enemy. Although I say, "I do not see the enemy," it does not mean that I do not see the enemy standing in front of me. To be able to see the one without seeing the other is a unique thing.

Therefore the true self is the self that existed before the separation of heaven and earth and before the birth of one's father and mother. This self is the self that is inside me, that is in the birds and the animals, the grass and the trees, and in all phenomena. It is exactly what is called the nature of the Buddha.

This self has no image or form, birth or death. It is not a self that can be seen with the physical eyes that you have in the present. Only a person who has received enlightenment can see it. A person who sees it is said to have grasped the essence of his true nature and become a Buddha.

....

*1. Personal view is a Buddhist term that means individual view that is based on the **erroneous** idea that the ego, or the personal self, constitutes a reality and can pick up things in a realistic way.*

A long time ago, the **World Honored One** went to the snowy mountains, and after spending six years of suffering there, received enlightenment.[2] This was the enlightenment of the **true self**. The ordinary man does not have power of faith and does not know what it means to persevere for even three or five years. However, those who study the Way persist with total

diligence for ten or twenty years, twenty-four hours a day. They develop tremendous power of faith, speak to people who possess wisdom, and ignore misfortune and suffering. Like a parent who has lost a child, they do not relax their determination one iota. They think profoundly, adding question upon question. In the end, they reach a place where even the Buddhist doctrine and Buddhist law simply dissolve, and they can see "this" naturally.

When I penetrate a place in which heaven and earth have not yet separated, where Yin and Yang have not yet been created, I necessarily gain an effect rapidly. This means turning one's gaze toward a place that existed before sky became sky and earth became earth, before Yin and Yang were created. The meaning is not to use thought or reason, but rather to look straight ahead. In this way, the arrival of the time in which a powerful effect will be achieved is assured.

---

2. *"The World Honored One" is one of the ten titles of Shakyamuni, the historic Buddha. The snowy mountains are the Himalayas.*

And thus, the expert uses the sword but does not kill others. He uses the sword and gives others life. When it is necessary to kill, he kills. When it is necessary to give life, he gives life. When he kills, he kills with absolute concentration. When he gives life, he gives life with absolute concentration. Without looking at right and wrong, he can see right and wrong. Without attempting to discriminate, he can discriminate well. Walking on water is exactly like walking on land, and walking on land is exactly like walking on water. If he is able to achieve this freedom, no man on earth can puzzle him. In every way, he will be beyond the need for companions.

The expert means the person who is an expert in martial arts.

He uses the sword but does not kill others means that even though he does not use the sword to kill others, when others face this principle, they retreat and become like dead people. There is no need to kill them.

He uses the sword and gives others life means that while he is fighting his opponent with the sword, he leaves everything to the opponent's movements and can observe him to his heart's content.

When it is necessary to kill, he kills. When it is necessary to give life, he gives life. When he kills, he kills with absolute concentration. When he gives life, he gives life with absolute concentration. The meaning of all this is whether he gives or takes life, he does it freely in a meditative state of total absorption and becomes one with the person in his mind at the time.

Without looking at right and wrong, he can see right and wrong. This means that he does not observe his martial art in order to say "right" or "wrong," but rather he can **see** right and wrong. He does not attempt to judge things, but he is capable of judging well.

When a mirror is set up in a certain place, the shape of whatever happens to stand in front of it will be reflected in it and be visible. Since the mirror does this mindlessly, the various forms will be reflected in it clearly without any intention of discriminating them from one another.

Since the person who engages in martial arts organizes his entire mind in the form of a mirror, he has no intention of discriminating right from wrong. However, in accordance with the clarity of the mirror of his mind, he sees the judgment regarding right and wrong without thinking about it.

Walking on water is exactly like walking on land, and walking on land is exactly like walking on water. The meaning of these words cannot be grasped by a person who has not achieved enlightenment about the very source of humankind.

If a foolish man walks on land like he walks on water, when he walks on land, he is liable to fall on his face. If he walks on water like he walks on land, when he actually enters the water, he is liable to think that he really can walk on it. Regarding this matter, the person who forgets about both land and water should arrive at this principle for the first time.

If he is able to achieve this freedom, no man on earth can puzzle him. The master of martial arts who achieved freedom will not be puzzled about the action he is required to take, no matter whom he encounters.

In every way, he will be beyond the need for companions. Since he will not have any equal in the world, he will be exactly like Shakyamuni, who said: "In heaven above and earth below, I alone am the Honored One." [3]

---

3. It is said that when Shakyamuni was born, he took seven steps in each of the four directions, pointed at the sky with his right hand, and uttered the sentence quoted above.

Do you want to achieve this? Walking, stopping, sitting or reclining, speaking or remaining silent, during tea and during rice, you must never neglect effort, you must quickly direct your gaze at the goal and investigate thoroughly, both "coming" and "going." In this way, you should look at things directly. As the months and years go by, this should resemble a light that appears alone in the dark. You will receive wisdom without a teacher and possess a mysterious ability without persevering. At precisely such a time, this is not unusual, but transcends the ordinary. I call this "Taia."

Do you want to achieve this? "This" indicates what was explained above, so that the question is whether you are considering achieving the essence of what was explained.

Walking, stopping, sitting or reclining. These four actions are called "the four dignities."[4] They occur in all human beings.

Speaking or remaining silent means when speaking about things or not saying anything.

During tea and during rice means when drinking tea and eating rice.

4. *The Buddhist concept mentions states in which the person inspires respect as a result of his conduct. The four states represent all the possible states of a human being, which, when calculated globally, reach the number of eighty thousand.*

You must never neglect effort, you must quickly direct your gaze at the goal and investigate thoroughly, both "coming" and "going." This means that you must never be careless or negligent in your efforts and you must always come back to yourself. You must quickly direct your gaze at the goal and constantly investigate those principles in depth. Always go straight forward, viewing what is right to be right and what is wrong to be wrong, and apply this principle to everything.

As the months and years go by, this should resemble a light that appears alone in the dark. This means that you must continue your efforts tirelessly just as described. The more you advance as time goes by, the more the acquisition of this mysterious principle by your own efforts will resemble a situation in which you suddenly encounter a lantern illuminating the dark night.

You will receive wisdom without a teacher means that you will gain fundamental wisdom without instruction from a teacher.

[You will] possess a mysterious ability without persevering. Since the ordinary person's actions all originate in his mind, they all belong to the world of created phenomena and therefore involve suffering. In parallel, actions that are uncreated stem from fundamental wisdom and are therefore natural and tranquil.[5]

---

5. *"Created phenomena" are formed as a result of the law of Karma.*
"Uncreated phenomena" are those that are independent of action, word or will.

At precisely such a time means at exactly such a time. The expression indicates the time at which the person receives wisdom without a teacher and possesses a mysterious ability without persevering.

This is not unusual, but transcends the ordinary. This means that this uncreated mysterious ability is formed from the unusual.

Since only actions that are ordinary and mundane by nature become "uncreated," this principle never exceeds or separates itself from the ordinary. In other words, the ordinary actions in the world of created phenomena of the ordinary, everyday person are completely different. Accordingly, it is said that "this is not unusual, but transcends the ordinary."

I call this "Taia." Taia is the name of an ancient Chinese sword that is unequaled anywhere on earth. This famous, jewel-encrusted sword can cut freely through anything from hard, tempered metal to hard, dense gemstones. There is nothing on earth that can parry the blade of this sword. The person who obtains this uncreated mysterious ability cannot be budged by huge armies or hundreds of thousands of enemy forces. This is the same as nothing being able to hinder the blade of this renowned sword. Therefore I call the power of this mysterious ability the **Taia sword**.

All people are equipped with this sharp Taia sword, which is perfectly complete for each of them. Those for whom this is clear are feared even by the Maras, but those for whom this is incomprehensible are deceived even by the heretics.[6] On the one hand, when two people of identical skill meet at swordpoint, it will be a duel without an outcome. This is like Shakyamuni holding the flower and the subtle smile of Kashyapa.[7] On the other hand, lifting the one and understanding the other three, or discerning fine differences in weight with the naked eye are examples of ordinary cleverness.[8] The person who masters this will quickly cut you in three before the one has been lifted and the three have been understood. How much more so when you encounter him face to face!

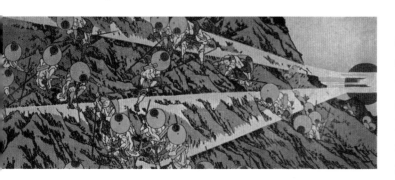

All people are equipped with this sharp Taia sword, which is perfectly complete for each one of them. This means that the famous Taia sword, which cannot be parried by the blade of any other sword in the world, is not just given to other people. Everyone, without exception, is equipped with it. It is neither missing or flawed for anyone – rather, it is perfectly complete.

6. A Mara is a demon. The literal meaning the Sanskrit word is "life stealer." The reference here is to the Deva Mara, who, from his seat in the Sixth Heaven, interferes with the practice of Buddhism.

7. Kashyapa (Mahakashyapa) the greatest ascetic of Buddhism's ten main disciples, became the disciples' leader after the Buddha's death.

8. The text here is unclear. From the grammatical point of view, it seems to compare the example of "the one and the three" to the reference to Shakyamuni and Kashayapa, but this does not correspond to either the overall meaning or to the development of the text.

This is a matter of the mind. Your mind was not born when you were born and will not die when you die. This being the case, it is said that the mind is your **original face.**[9] Heaven cannot cover it. Earth cannot support it. Fire cannot burn it and water cannot extinguish it. Even the wind cannot penetrate it. There is nothing in the world that can interfere with it.

Those for whom this is clear are feared even by the Maras, but those for whom this is incomprehensible are deceived even by the heretics. There is nothing in the universe that can obstruct the vision of a person who has received enlightenment about his **original face.** There are no means that can activate the Maras' supernatural power. Since the vision of such a person is so deeply penetrating that he can understand his own intentions, the Maras are afraid of him, avoid running into him and hesitate to approach him.

In contrast, the person who is unclear about his original face accumulates innumerable confused thoughts and delusions that subsequently cling to him. The heretics can easily deceive such a person.

---

9. *The reference to "the one and the three" evidently comes from the Confucian Analects (7:8): "The Master said, 'I do not enlighten those who are not enthusiastic, nor do I educate those who are not eager to learn. I do not repeat myself to those who – when I lift one corner – do not return to me after lifting the other three.'"*

When two people of identical skill meet at swordpoint, it will be a duel without an outcome. This means that if two people who have understood the nature of their original faces were to meet, draw their Taia swords and begin dueling, neither would win. This can be compared to the encounter between Shakyamuni and Kashayapa.

Shakyamuni holding the flower and the subtle smile of Kashyapa. At the gathering at the peak of Gridhrakuta, when Shakyamuni was dying, he held up a red lotus flower. He showed it to eighty thousand monks and they all remained silent. Only Kashyapa smiled. Knowing that Kashyapa had been enlightened at that time, Shakyamuni entrusted him with the Correct Doctrine, which does not rely on the written word and is passed on in a special way, without studying, and imprinted the Buddha seal on him.[10]

From that time on, the Correct Doctrine was transmitted over twenty-eight generations to Bodhidharma in India. In China, it was transmitted from Bodhidharma in six transmissions until it reached the Sixth Patriarch, Zen Master Ta Chien.[11] The latter became a bodhisattva, and from then on, Buddhist law thrived in China, its offshoots and branches rapidly growing and spreading and disseminating the **Five Houses and the Seven Sects,** and was finally

---

10. *The last part of the sentence is from the Pi Yen Lu, a collection of Zen problems, sayings and stories of the patriarchs. "Raising the one and understanding the three others, discerning the subtle differences in weight with the naked eye – these are the ordinary tea and rice of the Buddhist monk."*
11. *"Original face" is the pure nature of the mind that not yet been tainted by human intentions or mundane matters.*

transmitted to the Japanese priests Daio and Daito via the priest Nai Chih Hsu T'ang.[12] The Correct Doctrine continued to be transmitted uninterruptedly from teacher to pupil until this very day.

It is difficult to reach and decipher the doctrine of "holding the flower and the subtle smile" by means of guessing. In order to reach it, it is necessary to drink the breath of all the Buddhas while swallowing our own voice.

Although there is no way to express this principle, when pressed, it is possible to present the example of taking water from one vessel and pouring it into another vessel so that the water in the two vessels is mixed and cannot be distinguished. This is the moment in which Shakyamuni's and Kashyapa's eyes met and united. Relativity no longer exists.

Among all the masters of martial arts in every discipline there is not one in a hundred thousand who grasped the meaning of "holding the flower and the subtle smile." Be this as it may, if our intentions were extremely strong and our will to understand were especially powerful, then we would have to discipline ourselves for thirty more years. If we made a mistake, not only would we not master the martial arts, but we would enter hell like an arrow released from a bow. It really is frightening.

---

12. *The non-reliance on the written word and the passing on without studying are two points that are particularly stressed in Zen. They stress the principle that a person must look into the depths of his nature and not rely on texts or on what others teach.*

Lifting the one and understanding the other three means that the moment one part is shown, three others are immediately understood.

Discerning fine differences in weight with the naked eye means the function of the eye, or measuring by means of the eye.

Differences in weight are very fine.[13] The person who can use his eye to measure out any quantity of gold and silver without making any mistakes is clever and skilled.

[These] are examples of ordinary cleverness means that clever people like this are common and numerous, and therefore there is nothing special about them.

The person who masters this will quickly cut you in three before the one has been lifted and the three have been understood. This sentence concerns a person who has been enlightened as to the cause of the Buddha's appearance in the world. He will quickly cut you in three even before the one has been lifted and the three have been understood, or before any other indication appears. Therefore I suppose that when one meets someone like that, there is nothing one can do.

How much more so when you encounter him face to face! A person who has achieved speed and skill like that will cut a person he meets face to face with such ease that his opponent will not even know that he has been decapitated.

---

13. *Bodhidharma was the first patriarch of Ch'an (Zen) Buddhism in China. It is said that he came to China from India in either 470 or 520 CE. Ta Chien (37-713) was known by the name Hui Neng. He was a central figure in the development of Zen.*

Ultimately, such a person never exposes the tip of his sword. Its speed – even lightning cannot compete with it. It is even faster than a gale. If a person who does not have such tactics eventually becomes embroiled or confused, he will destroy his own sword or injure his own hand and his skill will fail. It is not possible to divine the secret of this ability by impressions or knowledge. It cannot be transmitted by words or speech, or learned through any doctrine. This is the law of the special transmission that goes beyond teaching.

Ultimately, such a person never exposes the tip of his sword. In other words, from the outset, a master will never show the tip of his sword.

Its speed – even lightning cannot compete with it. It is even faster than a gale. Regarding speed and technique, this means that even lightning, which is gone even before you think you saw it, cannot penetrate the movements of this man. Regarding the speed of the action, it disappears even more quickly than the fine grains of sand that are thrashed about during a gale.

If a person who does not have such tactics eventually becomes embroiled or confused means that without such skill, if a person is linked even slightly to lifting his sword or applying his mind…

...he will destroy his own sword or injure his own hand and his skill will fail. This means that he will certainly break the tip of his sword, injure his hand, and it is unlikely that he will ever be considered a skilled warrior.

It is not possible to divine the secret of this ability by impressions or knowledge. The words "impressions or knowledge" indicate knowledge and discrimination that occur in the human heart. **To divine** means to figure things out and unravel their meaning. In other words, your attempts to figure the secret of the ability out by impressions or knowledge are doomed to failure. Therefore, avoid figuring things out and trying to decipher them.

It cannot be transmitted by words or speech, or learned through any doctrine. For a true master of martial arts, this cannot be transmitted in words. Moreover, there is no doctrine that can teach which position to choose or where to strike.

This is the law of the special transmission that goes beyond teaching. It is not possible to transmit it in words or to teach it, no matter what method is used. Thus, it is called the doctrine of the "special transmission that goes beyond teaching." It is a doctrine that cannot be taught by a teacher. It requires self-enlightenment, and the learner has to become aware of its nature by himself.

There is no fixed rule regarding the manifestation of this tremendous ability. Orderly action, contrary action – even heaven does not determine this. If this is the case, what is the nature of this ability? In ancient times, people said, "When there is no painting of a Pai Che in the house, it is as if there were no ghosts at all." If a person has tempered himself and reached this principle, he will control everything under heaven with a single sword.

There is no fixed rule regarding the manifestation of this tremendous ability.[14] If the "tremendous ability" of the law of special transmission were to manifest itself in front of us, it would do so freely, without any rules. In parallel, the "tremendous ability" is so called because it extends in all directions and there is no place in which it is missing by even the tip of a rabbit's hair. A law is a rule or a regulation. There are no laws or regulations that can affect the manner in which this tremendous ability manifests itself.

Orderly action, contrary action – even heaven does not determine this.[15] The person who realizes this tremendous ability, whether he operates in an orderly way or a contrary way, is free and has no obstacles in his path.

---

14. *"The Five Houses and the Seven Sects" are the sects and sub-sects of Zen.*
15. *Daio Kokushi (1234-1308) was a monk from the Rinzai sect, which studied Buddhism in China. Daito Kokushi (1282-1337) was Daio's follower who was considered to be the founder of Zen at Daitokuji. Nai Chih Hsu T'ang (1185-1269) was also known by the name Hsu T'ang Chich Yu. He was a Chinese monk of Linchi Buddhism.*

What is the nature of this ability? Here is a situation in which we meet someone and ask him about the nature of a particular thing.

In ancient times, people said, "When there is no painting of a Pai Che in the house, it is as if there were no ghosts at all."

This is the answer to the previous question.

The Pai Che has a body of a cow and a human head, and does not resemble any other beast. It eats dreams and misfortunes, and in China its picture is painted and placed at the entrance to the house or hung on interior pillars. Briefly put, a painting of Pai Che is hung to thwart ill fortune.

A person who has not had ghosts in his house from the outset would not think of painting a picture of Pai Che and hanging it in his house.

In other words, a person who has developed an ability to follow an orderly or a contrary path, since heaven cannot determine what is in his mind, completely transcends pain and pleasure and does not suffer misfortunes either at home or in body.

For this reason, his mind will not yearn for a picture of Pai Che and his world will be beautiful.

If a person has tempered himself and reached this principle, he will control everything under the sun with a single sword. This means that a person who disciplines himself, completely tempering this pure metal a thousand times and immediately becoming free, like the sword that is drawn from its scabbard as fast as lightning, should resemble the founder of the Han dynasty and control everything under heaven with a single sword.

Those who study this must not be thoughtless. Those who study the mysterious principle of this sword must not glibly adopt thoughtless ideas, but must strive to intensify their own luster, to continue their tireless efforts, and not be negligent for even a moment.

Takuan Soho (1573-1645)

Art Appreciation

A long time ago, in a forest in China, there was a magnificent, majestic Kiri tree. It was so tall that its branches seemed to converse with the stars in the sky, and its coppery roots intertwined with the coils of the silver dragon that lived deep in the earth.

One day, a powerful wizard turned the tree into a fantastic harp, which he presented to the Emperor. It was a proud and stubborn harp, and could not be played by just anyone: only the most talented and intuitive musician would be able to master it. For years, the only sounds it emitted in response to people's attempts to play it were cacophonous and discordant, and it refused to accompany the songs they wished to sing.

Finally, after many years, the master harpist, Pai Ya, showed up. Instead of grabbing the harp and beginning to play, he held it gently and caressed it lovingly, his fingers rippling its strings. When he began to sing, his song was about nature and the seasons. These things resonated in the heart of the harp, and it responded to the musician's song. He sang of rivers, mountains, and the seasons – frolicking streams and tender flowers in the spring, the soothing buzz of insects and the sound of the falling rain in the summer, animal sounds, the glow of the moon's reflection on the frosty ground in the fall, and the whirling snow and hail in the trees in the winter.

Pai Ya then sang a love song about a lovesick youth and a proud young girl.

This was followed by the commotion of a battle scene with clashing weapons and horses. Finally, the dragon emerged from the bowels of the earth and stampeded through the mountains.

The emperor was entranced by the music, and asked Pai Ya how he had managed to discover the secret of the harp. The musician replied that he had not attempted to sing about himself; on the contrary, he had let the harp lead him to wherever it wanted to go, and in so doing, he and the harp had become one indistinguishable entity.

This is what art appreciation is all about. A real work of art appeals to our highest emotions. The artist – be he a painter, a musician, or an actor – reaches out to us and plays us as if we were his instrument or his canvas. We respond ecstatically to his touch. There is a meeting of the minds; we see things that cannot be seen and hear things that cannot be heard. The artist evokes memories, hopes and longings in vivid shades. His colors are our emotions; his use of light and dark is our joy or sorrow. We and the work of art are inextricably, indistinguishably linked.

During the Battle of Bungo

During the Battle of Bungo, Lord Takanobu received a gift of a barrel of sake from the enemy. About to open the barrel and drink, Takanobu was stopped by his henchmen, who warned that such a gift was probably poisoned. Takanobu listened to their argument, and then told them that whether the gift was poisoned or not would have very little effect on the battle. So saying, he opened the barrel, drank three big cups of sake in front of the messenger who had brought it, offered the messenger a cup, and sent him back to the enemy camp with a reply.

Akifusa, an unequalled warrior and swordsman, sought refuge from his former clan with Iesada. He had two brave and skilled retainers called Ingazaemon, and Fudozaemon, and they were with him all the time.

One day, Lord Takanobu sent a request to Iesada to kill Akifusa. While the latter sat on the porch with Ingazaemon washing his feet, Iesada hurried up behind him and cut his head off. Before his head fell off, however, Akifusa drew his sword and cut off Ingazaemon's head. The two heads fell into the basin, but then Akifusa's head rose up into the middle of the assembled company. This was an example of his magical talent.

Tannen the priest would say that a monk cannot realize the Buddhist way if he does not show compassion outwardly and gather courage inwardly. If a warrior does not show courage outwardly and store enough compassion inwardly to make his heart burst, he cannot become a retainer. For this reason, the monk uses the warrior as a role model for courage, and the warrior uses the monk as a role model for compassion.

Tannen went on to say that over many years, he met numerous wise men, but did not find the way to pursue knowledge. When he heard of a man of courage, he would go and find him, no matter how difficult the journey was. He realized that the stories about Way of

the Samurai were helpful on the path to Buddhism. An armed warrior can invade an enemy camp, using his armor as his strength. However, can a rosary-bearing monk armed with compassion and weakness rush into the battle arena? Not without a great deal of courage. This lack of courage can be seen in the priest who trembles when offering incense at a great Buddhist ceremony.

There are things that monks have to deal with – such as pulling all living creatures out of hell – that require courage. Be that as it may, monks nowadays no longer seek to gather courage, and prefer to be praised for their gentleness. These monks cannot complete the Way. Some warriors are cowards, and take shelter behind Buddhism. Young samurai must not learn about Buddhism because this will make them think about things in two ways rather than single-mindedly. Once a man is retired, he can begin to learn about Buddhism to occupy himself, but if a warrior carries the dual burden of loyalty and filial respect on one shoulder, and courage and compassion on the other, until he is worn out, he will not be a samurai.

When praying in the morning and the evening, and during the day, a man should chant his master's name, which is similar to chanting Buddha's names and holy words. He should be in harmony with the family's gods, because this strengthens his fate, like a mother's nurturing. The cruel warriors who were brave on their own are well known.

One day, one of Lord Naohiro's retainers stated that there was no man, besides himself, on whom his master could rely entirely. He was the only one who would die for him. This made Naohiro very angry, and he retorted that there was not one among his retainers who would be sorry to give up his life for him. Naohiro accused the man of being arrogant, and would have hit him if his cronies had not pulled him away.

One day, the founder of the Chiba family was sailing to Shikoku Island when a gale sprang up and damaged the boat. Thanks to a shoal of abalone crowding together and blocking up the holes in the boat, the boat did not sink. From that day on, no one in the Chiba family ever ate abalone again. If they did so inadvertently, it was said that their bodies were covered with abalone-shaped boils.

When the castle of Arima fell, Mitsuse Genbei sat himself down between two fields. The overseer passed by, saw him sitting there, and asked what he was doing. Genbei answered that he was suffering from abdominal pains that prevented him from taking another step. He told the overseer that he had sent his men on ahead, and asked him to take command. The overseer reported this event, and Genbei was ordered to commit seppuku. This is because abdominal pains were an indication of cowardice – they came on suddenly and made a person incapable of moving.

When Lord Naohiro died, Lord Mitsushige sent a message to Naohiro's estate, prohibiting his retainers from committing tsuifuku. This message was unacceptable to the retainers. However, Ishimaru Uneme, a young and relatively insignificant retainer, spoke up, apologized for his boldness, and supported Mitsushige's prohibition. He continued to say that although he had been brought up by Naohiro, and owed him his entire loyalty, he had been convinced by Mitsushige's reasoning and had decided to serve him, as Naohiro's successor. When the others heard this, they all decided to do the same.

At the end of a game of shogi played by two lords, Masaie and Hideyoshi, the obese Masaie attempted to stand up and take his leave. However, having knelt for a long time, he found that his feet were numb, and to the raucous amusement of the watching daimyo, he had to crawl away. He decided that, due to the inappropriate nature of the game for a person in his condition, he would no longer agree to play.

During the battle between Goto and Hirae on Kabashima island, Uemonnosuke was killed. Before leaving for the front, he had hugged his young son Shikibu and told him to win honor in the Way of the Samurai when he grew up. Shikibu himself would embrace his children and admonish them to be very strong and useful to their masters, even though they were too young to understand.

When Ogawa Toshikiyo's legitimate son died young, one youthful retainer committed seppuku.

When Taku Yasuyori died, Koga Yataemon committed tsuifuku, claiming that he had been unable to repay his master's kindness.

Bushido Shoshinsu

75

According to the Way of the Samurai

Not taking revenge is reprehensible. Revenge is breaking into a place and being killed. Once a person starts thinking about how to do it, time runs out. It is time-consuming to weigh up the pros and cons of attacking. Moreover, a person does this, he will ultimately reject the idea of revenge.

The important thing about revenge is resolve. Even if the person is hugely outnumbered, simply tackling one man after the other for as long as he can is very satisfying and often effective.

When Lord Asano was assassinated, his warriors waited a whole year for revenge on their lord's enemy, Lord Kira. They should have committed seppuku immediately. Their delay was a mistake.

According to the Way of the Samurai, there is no time to deliberate and work things out. The person should be forearmed with knowledge in order to be able to act immediately. Also, he has no idea what is going to happen, and must question everything all the time. Victory and defeat are transient and coincidental, but in order to avoid shame, death is the simplest answer.

Even if the odds are against you, you must fight back, regardless of knowledge or skill, or victory or defeat. Dive heedlessly into death, and you will wake up.

Hagakura

An eye-witness account of an act of *seppuku*

66**T**he seven of us foreign representatives were requested to follow the Japanese witnesses into the central hall of the temple – the hondo – where the ceremony was to take place. The room was impressive: spacious with a high ceiling supported by dark wooden pillars. Numerous golden lamps and other decorations that are typical of Buddhist temples hung from the ceiling. The floor in front of the high altar was raised a few inches from the ground and covered with lovely white mats. Near the altar was a red felt rug. The place was dimly lit with long candles, which created a mysterious atmosphere, and barely enabled us to see what was going on. The seven Japanese stood to the left of the low platform, while we foreigners stood to the right. We were the only ones there.

"After a few extremely tense moments, Taki Zenzaburo, a sturdy 32-year-old man who carried himself with great dignity, entered the hall. He was dressed in his ceremonial robes, including the strange wings that are only worn on the most important occasions. He was accompanied by four men: the kaishaku – who technically speaking was the executioner, but was more like a gentlemanly second in a duel; in fact, the role of kaishaku was frequently played by a relative or friend of the condemned man; and three officers, dressed in their uniform overcoat trimmed with gold. In this case, Taki Zenzaburo's kaishaku was one of his pupils, and had been chosen for the task by his peers because he was a superb swordsman.

"The kaishaku was on Taki Zenzaburo's left as the two of them approached the three officers and bowed to them. Then they approached us and bowed deeply to us, too – possibly even more respectfully. Both the officers and the foreigners returned the greeting. The condemned man stepped onto the platform slowly and with great dignity, prostrated himself in front of the altar twice, and knelt on his haunches on the red rug, his back to the altar. The kaishaku hunkered down to his left. At this point, one of the three officers came forward, holding a kind of offering-stand that contained the wakizashi – the Japanese short sword or dagger, about nine and a half inches long, which was wrapped in paper. The sword was pointed and razor-sharp. Bowing, he handed it to Taki Zenzaburo, who took it in both hands, lifted it to his head very respectfully, and then placed it on the rug in front of him.

"Taki Zenzaburo bowed deeply once again, and began his difficult confession. Neither his face nor his body language betrayed his deep emotion, but his hesitation and mixed feelings could be sensed in his voice.

"'I was the one – no one else – who unjustifiably gave the orders to fire on the foreigners at Kobe and then a second time when they attempted to escape. Because of this crime, I will disembowel myself. I hope that all of you who are present will do me the honor of witnessing my action.'

"He bowed once again, and let his robes fall to his waist, so that his upper torso was exposed. He tucked his sleeves under his knees, as was customary, so that he would not fall backward when he died – this would not be appropriate for a Japanese gentleman. With great determination, he grasped the dagger unflinchingly. He looked at it sadly, almost with love, and gathered his thoughts for the last time. Then he stabbed himself deeply below the waist on his left side and pulled the sword slowly to the right. He twisted it so that he could move it slightly upward. His face did not give the slightest indication of the pain involved in this ghastly procedure. Then he slowly pulled the sword out, leaned forward, and extended his neck. Although his face displayed a fleeting expression of pain, he remained absolutely silent. Now it was time for the kaishaku, who had watched Taki Zenzaburo's every move, to play his part: he leaped up, lifted his sword, steadied it, and brought it down with great force on the condemned man's neck. The sword flashed and there was a sound of something heavy falling. In one stroke Taki Zenzaburo had been decapitated.

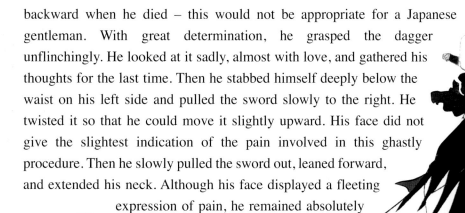

"There was absolute silence in the hall. The only sound that could be heard was the sickening gush of blood from the dead man's crushed body, which, only minutes before, had belonged to a courageous and dignified man. It was a horrible sight.

"The kaishaku bowed, cleaned the blade of his sword with a piece of paper he had prepared beforehand, and stepped off the platform. The bloodstained dagger was formally removed as evidence that the execution had taken place.

"We were then approached by the two representatives of the Mikado, who announced that Taki Zenzaburo's death sentence had been duly carried out. The ceremony was over, and we left the temple."

"When the three brothers – Sakon, 24, Naiki, 17, and Hachimaro, 8, were sitting in a row, ready to die, Sakon turned to Hachimaro and said: 'You

go first so that I can be sure you've done it correctly.' Hachimaro replied that since he had never seen any commit seppuku, he would prefer to watch his brothers do it first, and then he would be able to imitate their actions. Sakon and Naiki smiled through their tears and praised the little boy, saying that he was worthy of being their father's son. They had him kneel between them, and then Sakon plunged the dagger into his left side, below the waist. He told Hachimaro to watch what he was doing, and instructed him not to push the dagger too far in.

This would ensure that he did not fall backward. He also told him to keep his knees firmly together. Naiki followed suit and told Hachimaro to keep his eyes open so that he did not resemble a dying woman. He told him that if his strength ran out, and the dagger met with any resistance inside him, he should take courage and make every effort to draw the dagger across. Hachimaro watched his brothers die, and then stripped to the waist and calmly imitated his brothers' actions."

Mitford -Tales of old Japan

A lone, horseless samurai is not a samurai.

Yamamoto Jin'emon was in the habit of saying:

If you can comprehend one matter, you can comprehend eight.

False laughter shows a lack of self-esteem in a man and lechery in a woman.

It is important to look into the eyes of the person to whom you are speaking. You should greet your listener politely once, at the beginning of the conversation. If you do not look your listener in the eye, it indicates a lack of courtesy.

It is impolite to walk around with your hands in your pockets.

Books and so on should be discarded or burned after reading. While reading books is all very well for the Imperial Court, the men in the House of Nakano are expected to excel in martial exploits using an oak staff.

A lone, horseless samurai is not a samurai.

You can rely on a kusemono [a real man].

The ideal daily routine for a samurai is to get up at four a.m., bathe and do his hair, eat at sunrise, and go to bed when it gets dark.

Even if he has not eaten, a samurai must use a toothpick.

Hagakura

Giri

According to Lord Naoshige, giri is the most deeply felt emotion. It is not merely the sorrow one feels when a family member dies. Giri is the emotion that causes one to weep about a total stranger who lived many, many years ago.

One day, when Lord Naoshige was passing through Chiriku, he was informed that a man of over 90 lived there, and it might be a good idea for Naoshige to stop by and visit someone who was lucky to have lived so long. Naoshige disagreed. He claimed that this poor old man had no doubt witnessed the demise of many of his nearest and dearest, and therefore did not consider him to be lucky in the least.

In a conversation with his grandson, Lord Motoshige, Lord Naoshige said that every family line, be it high or low, eventually declines. It was no good trying to prevent this, because then the end would be even more humiliating. The end should be accepted willingly. This might even enable the family line to continue.

Go beyond the accepted idea

Good calligraphy is nothing more than avoiding careless mistakes, but this will do nothing to prevent one's handwriting from being boring and stilted. Go beyond the accepted idea. This concept must not just be applied to calligraphy, but to everything.

Two warriors were known to have continued certain bodily functions even after they had been beheaded. Even if a person is on his deathbed, he can last out for a few more days. If not, he is an inferior person. This according to Mitani Jokyu.

When you are responsible for delivering letters and other written items, keep hold of them and do not let them go even once. Hand them over to the recipient in person.

Hagakura

Principles of Warriors

The warriors' code consists of two kinds of principles, each subdivided into two categories: (1) ordinary principles, which are subdivided into the principles of knighthood and weaponry, and (2) emergency principles, which are subdivided into the principles of army and combat.

In the principles of knighthood, personal hygiene – washing feet and hands and bathing twice a day, shaving, and doing one's hair – features very strongly. In addition, the principles include dressing appropriately for the season and the situation, with long and short swords and fan tucked securely in the belt. The warrior is expected to deal with guests courteously, in accordance with their rank, always avoiding small talk. His table manners should always be impeccable.

If the warrior is in public service and has some time off, this should be spent doing useful things such as practicing calligraphy or studying ancient stories or warrior codes. No matter what the warrior is doing, he must conduct himself in the manner of a true warrior.

The principles of weaponry require mastery of swordsmanship, and other martial arts such as archery, riding, lancing, shooting, and so on. The warrior must be so adept at these skills that he can use them whenever the need arises.

Mastery of the ordinary principles is suitable for regular employment and everyday life. When an emergency arises, however, this is when the warriors really come into their own. They discard their knightly conduct and assume military conduct toward their superiors, equals, and subordinates; they take off their suits, put on armor, take up their weapons, and set out to do battle. There are many ways of doing so, and these are known as army principles. Every warrior must be familiar with them.

Combat principles are basically the maneuvers and plans that either win or lose the battle. They are secrets that must be familiar to every warrior.

Together, army and combat principles constitute the emergency principles.

When a warrior has mastered the two kinds of principles and their subdivisions, he is a top-class knight. If he has only mastered the ordinary principles, he can serve as a knight, but without the emergency principles, he cannot be a samurai commander, a magistrate, a group leader, and so on.

In order to be a top-class warrior, both kinds of principles and their subdivisions must be mastered and practiced.

Bushido Shoshinshu

if you want to take revenge

A band of eight samurai went off to have a good time. Two of them decided to go to a teahouse, where they got into an argument and were thrashed by the men working there. The other six, who were enjoying themselves in a boat, heard the commotion, and three of them resolved to go and avenge their comrades. The other three objected, however, and dissuaded them from doing so, claiming that the incident would cause everyone trouble. The two samurai who had been in the fight managed to kill their opponents despite being heavily wounded. The samurai were severely reprimanded by their master upon their return.

The incident was carefully analyzed. Somebody claimed that if you want to take revenge, you cannot wait around and work out the pros and cons with all the other people. Revenge will never happen in this way. You must be resolved and then go out and do it. This same person also stated that a lot of big talk about revenge but no action is nothing but hypocrisy – a kind of covering yourself by talking so that later on you'll come out looking good. A truly brave person makes up his mind, says nothing, and goes out to fight. Even if he does not achieve his aim of killing the opponent, and is killed himself, he is still brave. However, a person who acts in this way will probably achieve his aim.

Hagakura

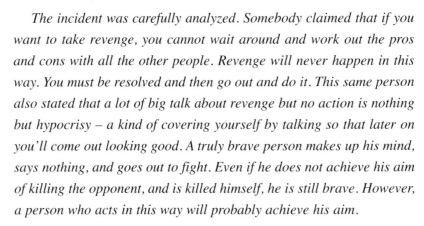

Military Equipment

It is essential for knights in public service to possess weapons and military equipment in accordance with their status. The equipment includes the items that are laid down in the military codes of the particular house as well as the ones that are stipulated by the employer: helmet crests as well as individual, spear, sleeve and carrier emblems. The employer is responsible for providing these recognition emblems. It is no use trying to hand them out for the first time when an emergency occurs; the fact that the employer has neglected his duties toward his employees up till now will be exposed, and this will reflect very badly on him. If his men are killed for failing to wear these recognition emblems, their deaths will be futile.

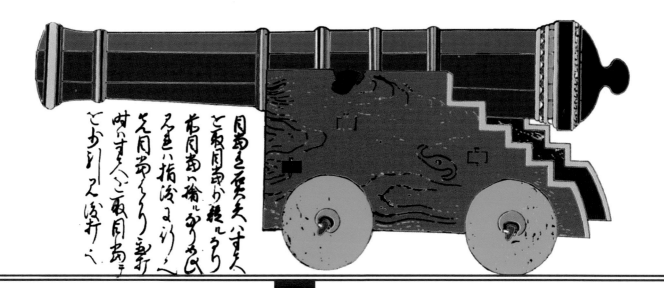

It is unforgivable for an employer to give his servants swords with wooden or bamboo blades because he assumes that they will never have to fight. It is equally unforgivable for him to permit them to eschew the use of loincloths – what if they have to gird their loins one day?

These things are even more applicable to a knight who is being paid for public service. Even if he does not fight a single battle all his life, it is imperative for him to be fully equipped. If he is not, his negligence is inestimably worse than the servants who carry wooden swords or do not wear loincloths.

In order to avoid the negligence mentioned above, the lower-ranking warrior should consider this: if he is prepared to spend three gold pieces on equipping himself, two of them should be spent on armor and helmet, and the third on all the other gear: underwear, trousers, tunic, coat, battle jacket, chaps, fan, whip, gear bag, mess kit, water bottle, and so forth. In other words, the "lesser" items are just as important as the armor.

Since the weight of the armor can be a tremendous stumbling-block if one is tired, wounded, or getting on in years, the warrior should not purchase heavy armor, even if he is in the bloom of youth and health. Think ahead. The same goes for thick metal banners – if the warrior purchased these when he was young and strong, and everyone identifies him because of them, it is very difficult to discard them when he is older and weaker. Again, think ahead!

Daimyo House Codes

Do not give a command post or an administrative position to anyone who lacks ability, even if his family has served the Asakura family for generations.

Post intelligence agents in both near and distant provinces, even if the world may be at peace. In so doing you can spy on the conditions of these domains without interruption.

Do not excessively covet swords and daggers made by famous masters. Even if you own a sword or dagger worth 10,000 pieces, it can be overcome by 100 spears each worth 100 pieces. Therefore, use the 10,000 pieces to procure 100 spears, and arm 100 men with them. You can in this manner defend yourself in time of war.

Those retainers who lack special talent or positions, but who are steadfast must be treated with compassion and understanding. Those who are effeminate may still be used as attendants or messengers if their demeanor is outstanding, and they must not be dismissed lightly. However, if they lack both, then it is useless to retain them.

Regrettable is the practice of selecting an auspicious day or considering a lucky direction in order to win a battle or take a castle, and even shift the time and date accordingly. No matter how auspicious the day may be, if you set sail your boat in a storm or confront a great host alone, your effort will come to naught. No matter how inauspicious the day may be, if you can discern between truth and falsehood, prepare for the orthodox and surprise attacks secretly, be flexible in all situations, and depend on a good stratagem, then your victory is assured.

Toshikage Jushichikajo 1480

Don't think your swords and clothes should be as good as those of other people. Be content as long as they don't look awful. Once you start acquiring what you don't have and become even poorer, you'll become a laughingstock.

Whenever you have a little bit of time for yourself, read a book. Always carry something with characters written on it with you and look at it when no one's looking. Unless you accustom yourself to them, asleep or awake, you'll forget them. The same is true of writing.

There's they saying, "Do everything with others, and you'll have no trouble." Rely on others in everything.

When you have to walk past the elders lined up in the corridor for the master's audience, you must bend at the hips and lower your hands. It's absolutely out of the question not to show deference or humility but to stomp past. All samurai must behave humbly, deferentially.

Always work at reading, writing, martial skills, archery, and horse riding. There is no need to detail this. Hold literary skills in your left hand, martial skills in your right. This is the law from ancient times. Never neglect it.

Soun-ji Dono Nijuichi Kajo 1495

In dealing with those who have quarreled, both parties should be sentenced to death, irrespective of who is in the right or in the wrong. In cases where one party to the dispute, although provoked and attacked, controls himself, makes no defense and, as a result, is wounded his appeal should be granted. While it is reprehensible that he should have been a party to the dispute and perhaps contributed to its outbreak, his respect for the law in not returning the attack merits consideration. However, in cases where warriors come to the aid of one or other parties to a dispute and then claim to be an injured party, their claims shall not be entertained, even if they should be wounded or killed.

Imagawa Kana Mokuroku 1526

Without a secret understanding with the daimyo, no one is permitted to send messages and letters to another province. However, of necessity, communications by the samurai residents of the Province of Shinano may be continued, as long as they are known to us to be engaged in devising a stratagem. Those who live on the border, who are accustomed to exchanging letters, need not be prohibited from doing so.

Anyone who marries outside of the province, by contracting to take possesion of another's estate, or to send his retainers for the service of another, creates the causes for a great disturbance. Therefore, such a marriage is strictly forbidden. If anyone disobeys this injunction, a severe admonishment shall be rendered.

Exchanging oaths privately by relatives and retainers is tantamount to treason. However, on the battlefield, it is permissible to enter into a compact, so as to encourage loyalty.

Pay proper reverence to the gods and the Buddha. When your thoughts are in accord with the Buddha's, you will gain more power. If your domination over others issues from your evil thoughts, you will be exposed, you are doomed. Next, devote yourselves to the study of Zen. Zen has no secrets other than seriously thinking about birth-and-death.

Koshu Hatto no Shidai 1548

Taking and keeping the landholdings of others is the worst kind of unlawful act. Those who have taken the domains of others should return them immediately to the lawful proprietor. When such domains are not returned voluntarily, the Daimyo shall order their return. If an order of this kind is not complied with, he shall order his retainers to expel the offender by force. In such cases the retainers must act cooperatively together as a single group in aid of the Daimyo. Even though the offender may be someone with whom they have close ties, a relative, or someone whom it is difficult to ignore, retainers are forbidden to go to the aid of the lawbreaker. On the other hand, even if the one whose lands have been taken is disliked by the retainers, insofar as the Daimyo orders, they must put aside their resentment and cooperate fully and actively in chastising the offender.

It is forbidden for the Daimyo to hand down and enforce a judgment in a trial without a full enquiry or without allowing the defendants an opportunity to explain the circumstances.

Rokkaku-shi Shikimoku 1567

I t should be the primary concern of everyone to train himself unceasingly in military accomplishment. Those who tend to excel their fellows in this should be given additional income. Particular attention should be paid to musketry, archery, and horsemanship. The military code is contained in a separate document.

It is only natural that services are demanded of those who hold fiefs, and they must be carried out to the letter regardless of whether they are large or small. Anyone late for logging or construction work will be required to repeat the duty period as punishment. And anyone who comes short of the food and provisions requested of him for work detail will be required to supply as much again.

In regard to those who abscond: offenders must be punished whatever their excuse and so also their relatives. Proper reward should be given neighbors or friends who report anyone whose behavior causes suspicion that he is planning to desert. Those who have knowledge of such intent and fail to report it will receive the same punishment as the offender. Furthermore, a man who reports late for lumbering or construction and leaves without getting permission from the magistrate will have his lands declared forfeited. If a man deserts directly to another province, punishment will also be imposed on his relatives. Similarly, if a man's retainer deserts, the master will be penalized threefold.

Heavy drinking is prohibited for all people, high and low, to say nothing of all magistrates. Furthermore: With regards to drunkards, the fine for minor offenses will be three kan of coins, and appropriate punishment will be imposed for severe offenses. A man who cuts or strikes others will have his head cut off.

As to illicit relations with another's wife: Although it is obvious, unless the guilty pair kill themselves, both of them should be executed. If approval of relatives is obtained, revenge may be undertaken, but unnatural cruelty will constitute a crime. If the husband fails to kill the man, or if he is away at the time the offense becomes known, the people of the village should kill the offender. In addition: If a woman has a reputation, the marriage contract is to be broken.

When there is not a man in the house, no males-masseurs, peddlers, traveling sarugaku performers and musicians, solicitors for religious contributions or even relatives-shall set foot in the house. If someone is ill and if the relatives approve, a visit may be made, but then only in daytime. Even the magistrate must carry on his business outside the gate. However, this does not apply to parents, sons, and brothers of the household head.

Whoever discovers that anyone, whether vassal or farmer, is concealing the existence of fields and reports it to the lord, will be rewarded strikingly. Acting on such information, the magistrate will base his ruling on the land survey register. If it becomes clear that a vassal concealed the field, he will be severely punished. And if it is a farmer who concealed it, he will be forced to pay double the tax due since the land survey, after which he will be banished. If he pleads hardship at this, he will have his head cut off.

With regard to family succession: It is necessary to notify the lord and receive his permission, even if the heir is the head's real child. It is strictly forbidden to decide succession matters privately. Furthermore: One must also request permission to become guardian for a minor.

As regards family name and succession designation for loyal retainers: If a vassal commits a crime and has to be punished, his family name will not be affected if the offense was a minor one. But if he commits a major crime, his punishment should include the loss of his family name.

Chosokabe-shi Okitegaki **1596**

G reater and lesser lords are strictly prohibited from entering deliberately into contracts and from signing oaths and the like.

If there is a fight or quarrel, the one who exercises forbearance will be favored.

Concerning the management of fiefs throughout the country: after the crops have been inspected, the lord should take two-thirds and the farmer one-third. In any case, orders should be issued which will ensure that the fields do not become devastated.

One of lesser status may keep, in addition to his principal wife, one handmaid, but he should not maintain a separate house. Even one of greater status should not exceed one or two concubines.

Conform to the limitations of your fief; in all things your actions should be consistent with your standing.

Osaka jochu kabegaki **1595**

A single word

Every single word is of great importance to a samurai, regardless of the circumstances. A single word can demonstrate bravery in battle, in times of unrest as well as in times of peace. It can also show strength or betray cowardice. Every single word emanates from the heart, and is not just uttered by the mouth.

If one has a firm basis, unexpected deviations from small details or matters will not be of great importance. However, details must not be ignored. They are the elements that make the things one does right or wrong.

Hagakura

Oda Nobunaga

T he acquisition of knowledge pertaining to the use of firearms, especially guns, and the rapid application of the new technology characterized the "victorious" Japan as early as the 16th century. The best example of this was Oda Nobunaga, the daimyo who united Japan under his rule in the second half of the 16th century and became the most senior samurai.

In the middle of the 16th century, the Portuguese introduced the guns that were common at the time in Europe into Japan. These guns were clumsy, loading them was a complicated and very time-consuming process, and it was sometimes necessary to wait several minutes between shots in order to allow the metal parts to cool down. Moreover, the guns were inaccurate, and the metal or stone bullets they shot were lethal only at a distance of a few dozen yards; beyond this distance, the bullets did not penetrate the warriors' armor. An expert archer – and the samurai were first and foremost expert archers – could shoot a dozen arrows in the time it took for a gunman to release one shot from his gun. Furthermore, the samurai's arrows were more accurate than the bullets of the time, and had a greater range.

However, Oda Nobunaga understood what other daimyos did not understand: the effective operation of a bow required a skilled, fit, and experienced samurai warrior. The bow was effective as a weapon in the hands of the elite of the Japanese warrior class, be it the bow that was used while the warrior was standing up, or – especially – the bow that was used while

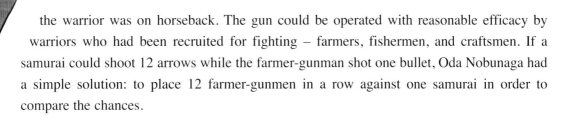

the warrior was on horseback. The gun could be operated with reasonable efficacy by warriors who had been recruited for fighting – farmers, fishermen, and craftsmen. If a samurai could shoot 12 arrows while the farmer-gunman shot one bullet, Oda Nobunaga had a simple solution: to place 12 farmer-gunmen in a row against one samurai in order to compare the chances.

Oda Nobunaga turned the regiments of farmer-gunmen into a genuine fighting force, and this force helped him and the samurai under his control to break the deadlock that had prevailed until that time between the warring rulers.

The interesting thing is that Oda Nobunaga did not "invent" the principle that induced him to adopt firearms. The same idea appeared in many kahos that had been written before his time. (A kaho was a collection of house or tribal rules compiled by daimyos, which became the mandatory rules of conduct.) In a 15th-century kaho we find the following clause:

> *"He (the samurai) must not become addicted to swords and weapons whose reputation precedes them. Even if the samurai has a sword that is worth one thousand coins, it will not overcome one hundred warriors bearing spears, each of which is worth ten coins. Therefore it is preferable for him to purchase (for the cost of the sword) one hundred spears, and equip one hundred warriors with spears, and thus he can head a division of warriors."*

The First Guns

The first Westerners to reach Japan did so by chance in the early years of the 1540s, when a storm drove a Chinese junk carrying three Portuguese passengers on to Tanegashima island, near southern Kyosho. The Japanese were fascinated not only by their physical appearance and attire, but – especially – by their guns. This fascination grew into something of an obsession when the daimyo of Kyosho, Lord Tokitada, witnessed the shooting of a duck. He had to learn to use these weapons, and even more so, he had to possess them. He did both within a month, and paid a fortune for the guns.

He instructed his swordsmith, Yatsuida, to take the guns and copy them. He had no problem reproducing the barrel, but the more intricate parts stymied him. The secret was revealed to him some time later by a Portuguese gunsmith, who demanded Yatsuida's teenage daughter in exchange for the information.

Lord Tokitada sold the many guns produced by Yatsuida to other military leaders, and a decade later, high-quality guns were being produced countrywide. They were popular weapons, since they could be manufactured quickly and inexpensively, and it did not take

long to train the ashigaru – the infantry – to use them skillfully. However, the gun's possibilities were not lost on the samurai, Takeda Shingen, who instructed his commanders in 1571 to increase the number of guns in their regiments. He was convinced that guns were the weapons of the future that would render spears and bows and arrows obsolete. How did Shingen die two years later? From a bullet!

According to the priest Ryoi

According to the priest Ryoi, samurai despised the idea of dying in bed rather than in battle. He felt that priests, too, could not fulfill their vocation if they did not think in the same way. The person who withdraws from society and shuns human company is a coward, and it is foolish and harmful to think that such a person who accomplishes any good. Even if he does do some good, it will be limited, because he is not out there disseminating the family traditions.

The gods do not protect a person who does not want to be killed by enemy arrows. However, a person who does not want to be struck by the arrows of a common soldier but rather by those of a renowned warrior, will be granted that protection.

Hagakura

Fame

In the famous ancient books, as well as in battle records, it is worthwhile noting that only the names of warriors who somehow distinguished themselves in battle are mentioned, while the hundreds or thousands of general casualties are simply mentioned as totals. While the warriors whose military accomplishments gained them a mention in the records might have been of lesser rank, many of the unnamed casualties might have been important top-rank warriors who did not do anything deserving of mention.

Think about this: The pain of losing your head is the same whether you died in a blaze of glory or whether the enemy cut your head off when you weren't looking. If this is the case, you should adopt the approach of "If I'm going to die anyway, I might as well be a hero and do some dashing deeds before forfeiting my head. In this way, I'll be a credit to my superiors as well as to future generations."

The warriors whose cowardice prompts them to remain in the rear, to take cover behind fellow warriors, or to retreat first, only to be killed by a stray arrow or by friendly fire – a futile loss of life – these men die an ignoble, shameful and useless death. There is nothing worse.

Kamikazi

In the West, the term kamikazi is known mainly from World War II, when Japanese pilots took off on long-range flights in planes loaded with explosives, without fuel for the return flight to their bases. Their mission was to crash into American warships or military bases. These suicide pilots boasted the name "kamikazi," and the word became the accepted name for suicide fighters.

In fact, the term kamikazi means "divine wind" or "wind sent by God." In 1281, Kublai Khan, the renowned Mongolian general, mustered a vast army, loaded his warriors onto ships, and prepared to invade and conquer the islands of Japan. The opposing samurai, although united against the foreign enemy, were not strong enough to halt the invasion.

Fortunately for the Japanese, a three-day gale intercepted the invading forces. The gale dispersed the Mongol fleet, causing many ships to crash into the rocks near the shore, which resulted in the watery death of the warriors who were sailing on them. The only thing left for the samurai to do was to attack the warriors who managed to reach the shore (most of them devoid of weapons and horses) and eliminate them.

The storm that sank the Mongols was named "kamikaze." According to the story, the wind was sent by the sun goddess, Amaterasu, at the behest of the emperor Kameyama. From then on, warriors who were prepared to surrender their lives while attacking an external enemy were called "kamikaze."

Famous Samurai

ADACHI TOKIAKI, Advisor to Hojo Takatoki

ADACHI YASUMORI, Shogun of Higo Provence (D. 1285)

AKAMATSU MITSUSUKE, Ashikaga period Shogun and the assassin of Shogun Ashikaga Yoshinori (D. 1441)

AKECHI MITSUHIDE, Oda Retainer and Destroyer of Nobunaga (1526 - 1582)

AMAKO AKIHISA, Amako Daimyo (1514 - 1562)

AMAKO TSUNEHISA, 1st Daimyo of the Amako (or Amago) (1458-1541)

ANAYAMA BEISETSU, One of Takeda 'Shingen's '24 Generals' (1532 - 1582)

ANKOKUJI EKEI, Advisor to the Mori Daimyo (D. 1600)

ARIMA HARUNOBU, Daimyo of Shimabara (D.1612)

ASAI NAGAMASA, Daimyo of omi (1545 - 1573)

ASHIKAGA TADAYOSHI, Brother of Ashikaga Takauji (D. 1352)

ASHIKAGA TAKAUJI, Founder of the Ashikaga Shogunate (1305 - 1358)

ASHIKAGA YOSHIAKI, 15th and final Ashikaga Shogun (1537 - 1597)

BABA NOBUFUSA, Mino no Kami; one of 'Shingen's 24 Generals' (1514 - 1575)

CHOSOKABE MOTOCHIKA, Daimyo of Tosa (1539 - 1599)

DATE MASAMUNE, Lord of Date family, son of Terumune (1566 -1636)

DATE TERUMUNE, Lord of Date family (1543 - 1585)

FUKUSHIMA MASAMORI, Toyotomi, Tokugawa retainer (1561 - 1624)

GOTO MOTOTSUGU, Toyotomi retainer (1573 - 1615)

HASHIBA HIDENAGA, Hideyoshi's half-brother and a chief retainer (1540 - 1591)

Amako Tsunehisa

Anayama Beisetsu

HATTORI HANZO, Tokugawa retainer and reputed 'ninja' leader (1541 - 1596)

HOJO SOUN, First Hojo Daimyo (1432 - 1519)

HOJO TOKIMASA, The 1st Hojo Regent (1138 - 1215)

HOJO TOKIMUNE, Hojo Regent (D. 1284)

HOJO UJIYASU, 3rd Hojo Daimyo (1515 - 1571)

HOJO UJIMASA, 4th Hojo Daimyo (1538 - 1590)

HONDA TADAKATSU, Tokugawa General (1548 - 1610)

HOSOKAWA FUJITAKA, Ashikaga, Oda, Toyotomi, Tokugawa retainer and noted scholar (1534 - 1610)

HOSOKAWA TADAOKI, Toyotomi, Tokugawa retainer, son of Fujitaka (1564 -1645)

HOSOKAWA YORIYUKI, Hosokawa lord and Asakura general (1329 -1392)

IKEDA NOBUTERU, Oda, Toyotomi retainer (1536 - 1584)

IKEDA TERUMASA, Toyotomi, Tokugawa retainer; 1st Ikeda daimyo (1564 - 1613)

IMAGAWA SADAYO, Tandai of Kyushu (1325 - 1420)

IMAGAWA YOSHIMOTO, Daimyo of Suruga and Totomi (1519 - 1560)

IRIKI-IN SHIGETOMO, Shimazu Vassal (D. 1544)

ISHIKAWA KAZUMASA, Tokugawa retainer (1534 - 1609)

KAJIWARA KAGETOKI, Supporter of Minamoto Yoritomo (d.1200)

KAKIZAKI KAGEIE, Uesugi retainer (d.1575)

KATO KIYOMASA, Toyotomi, Tokugawa general (1562 - 1611)

KIKKAWA MOTOHARU, Mori general (1530 - 1586)

KITABATAKE CHIKAFUSA, Emperor Go-Daigo's Chief Advisor (D.1354)

KOBAYAKAWA HIDEAKI, Toyotomi retainer (1577 - 1602)

KÛKI YOSHITAKA, Oda, Toyotomi general/admiral (1542 -1600)

KURODA YOSHITAKA, Toyotomi and Tokugawa retainer; also known as
Kanbei (1546-1604)

Chosokabe Motochika

KUSUNOKI MASASHIGE, Supporter of Emperor Go-Daigo's (1294 -1336)

MATSUNAGA HISAHIDE, Notorious schemer, and alternately ally and enemy of
Nobunaga (1510 - 1577)

MINAMOTO NORIYORI, Minamoto general and brother of Yoritomo and
Yoshitsune (1156 - 1193)

MINAMOTO YOSHIIE, Legendary warrior and hero of the 'later three-year war'
(1041-1108)

MINAMOTO YOSHITSUNE, Legendary Minamoto general (1159 -1189)

MIYAMOTO MUSASHI, Noted swordsman, author of Gorin no sho (1584? - 1645)

MIYOSHI KIYOTSURA, Confucianist Scholar-Statesman (847 - 918)

MOGAMI YOSHIAKI, Daimyo of Dewa (1546-1614)

MORI MOTONARI, Daimyo of Aki (1497 - 1571)

MORI TERUMOTO, Daimyo of the Mori Clan; Grandson of Mori Motonari (1553 - 1625)

NITTA YOSHISADA, Proponent of Emperor Go-Daigo (1301 - 1338)

ODA NOBUNAGA, Daimyo of Owari and the first of the "Three Unifiers" (1534 - 1582)

OIE MASAFUSA, Celebrated Heian Scholar (D. 1111)

OMURA SUMITADA, Daimyo of Hizen and the first Christian Daimyo (1532 - 1587)

OTOMO SORIN, Daimyo of Bungo (1530-1587)

OÛCHI YOSHIHIRO, Shogun of Suo and Nagato (1356 -1399)

SAICHO, Founder of the Enryaku-ji Monastery (767 - 822)

SAKIKABARA YASUMASA, Tokugawa General (1548 - 1606)

SANADA MASAYUKI, Takeda retainer, Daimyo of Ueda (1544 - 1608)

SATAKE YOSHISHIGE, Daimyo of Hitachi (1547 -1612)

SHIBATA KATSUIE, Oda Retainer and Rival of Toyotomi Hideyoshi (1530 - 1583)

SHIMAZU YOSHIHISA, Daimyo of Satsuma and Osumi (1533 - 1611)

TAIRA MUNEMORI, Son of Taira Kiyomori and head of the Taira clan (1147 - 1185)

Hojo Soun

Oda Nobunaga

TAKAYAMA UKON, The Christian Samurai (1552 - 1615)

TAKEDA KATSUYORI, 3rd and Final Daimyo of the Takeda of Kai (1546 - 1582)

TAKEDA SHINGEN, Lord of Kai (1521 - 1573)

TAKEZAKI SUENAGA, Warrior During Mongol Invasions

TOKUGAWA IEYASU, 1st Tokugawa shogun (1543-1616)

TOYOTOMI HIDEYOSHI, Unifier of Japan, Kampaku (1536 - 1598)

UESUGI KENSHIN, Lord of Echigo (1530 - 1578)

UKITA NAOIE, Daimyo of Bizen (1530 - 1582)

YAMAGATA MASAKAGE, One of Takeda Shingen's '24 Generals' (1524? - 1575)

YAMAMOTO KANSUKE, One of Takeda Shingen's '24 Generals'
(1501-1561)

YAMANAKA SHIKANOSUKE, Amako Retainer (1545 - 1578)

Kuroda Yoshitaka

Warrior Dolls

Kusonoki Masashige was a brilliant warrior who employed amazing stratagems to defend the Chihaya fortress against its innumerable enemies and undermine their morale. He had his men construct 24 life-size figures and dress them in full armor and weapons. During the night, the dummies were placed in front of the walls, concealing skilled archers. When the sun came up, Kusonoki's warriors yelled war-cries in order to get the Hojo forces to attack the forces stationed in front of the fortress. The Hojo warriors surged forward, but were mowed down by a sea of arrows from the concealed archers. The Hojo pressed forward to attack the dummies, and the archers retreated behind the walls. In the meantime, scores of boulders were dropped onto the Hojo from the top of the walls, killing and maiming hundreds of them. After the battle, the Hojo survivors realized to their horror that the "warriors" who had wrought such havoc on their fellow warriors were dummies. This meant that the troops who had perished under the weight of the boulders had died in vain, and without any glory!

Cold or bad weather

The way to avoid being affected by the cold or by bad weather is to attach several packages of cloves next to your body. The effectiveness of this is illustrated by the elderly Nakano Kazuma, who served as a messenger in bitterly cold weather, but accomplished his mission unscathed, thanks to the cloves. In order to staunch the flow of blood from an injury sustained by falling off a horse, you should drink a beverage made from the droppings of a spotted horse.

Hagakura

Muraoka no Goro and Hakamadare:
Never let your guard down

In his capacity as a super-mugger, Hakamadare was well known to the law-enforcement authorities, who succeeded in arresting him every now and then. Once, as luck would have it, the emperor pardoned certain types of criminals, and Hakamadare and a bunch of his cronies were released from prison. With nowhere to go and nothing to do, Hakamadare had a brainwave. He reached the Osaka Barrier, a checkpoint on Mount Osaka between Shiga and Kyoto, stripped, and lay down naked at the side of the road, seemingly lifeless.

It didn't take long for a crowd to gather around the "dead" man, staring at him and arguing about the cause of his death. Since there was no wound, they were completely mystified as to the nature of this guy's demise.

All of a sudden, an obviously high-ranking warrior, surrounded by a retinue of armed guards and servants, approached from the Kyoto direction. Curious about the crowd at the side of the road, he sent one of his guards to find out what the commotion was about. The guard returned and informed him that there was a man lying at the side of the road, ostensibly uninjured but dead nevertheless.

When the warrior heard the explanation, he barked an order to his retinue, spurred his horse, and took off at full speed. As he passed the "corpse," he gave it a quick glance. The crowd saw this cowardly behavior and began to laugh and scoff loudly at the so-called warrior and his band of armed guards. The jeers were audible long after the retinue had disappeared.

It wasn't long before the dead man lost his appeal, and the crowd dispersed, leaving Hakamadare lying alone and naked at the side of the road. Some time later, a lone warrior rode up to the corpse, and, without thinking, poked at him with his bow, wondering aloud how the poor guy had croaked, without a wound in evidence. Hakamadare, in a miraculous return from the dead, seized the bow, jumped up, and yanked the warrior off his horse and onto the ground. He grabbed the warrior's sword and stabbed him to death, yelling that this was the way to avenge his ancestors. Then he divested the warrior of his trouser-skirt, got dressed, took the weapons, mounted the horse, and sped off as fast as he could.

Hakamadare repeated this strategy several dozen times, until he had enough clothing, weapons, and horses to equip all of his jailbird cronies who had been released along with him, and were waiting for him in Kyoto. The disreputable band rode away and heaven help anyone who got in their way.

The moral of the story is that you have to be on your guard all the time. Even an innocent-looking dead body should be avoided, otherwise it might just spring to life and kill and rob you. The "cowardly" warrior who had steered clear of the corpse at the side of the road turned out to be the wily and alert Muraoka no Goro, who was aware of all the tricks, and did not let his guard down for a second. The lone warrior, on the other hand, was an idiot for being so careless.

The Warrior Monks

The golden age of the sohei, or warrior monks, lasted from the end of the ninth century to the seventh decade of the 16th century.

The history of these monks began in the eighth century, when a monk named Saicho established the Enryaku-ji monastery on Mount Hiei, northeast of Japan's new capital, Kyoto. In 804, the emperor, Kammu, sent Saicho to China to study various currents of Buddhism and to select the one most suitable for Kyoto. He opted for Tendai Buddhism, which he and his followers disseminated in the form of mystical ceremonies intended to foster health, prosperity, longevity, and good fortune – a perfect formula for success. As the protector of Kyoto, the monastery was highly respected.

However, the idyllic situation was brutally disrupted at the end of the ninth century when the followers of two Tendai instructors clashed and set up separate establishments – one at Enryaku-ji and one at Miidera. The rivalry did not end here – there was also animosity between the Tendai and other Buddhists sects. Spiritual issues became entangled with the materialistic aspects of protecting their wealth from covetous samurai and tax officials. To this end, the Tendai began to employ armies of warrior monks, or sohei. This quickly became the accepted practice for religious institutions.

It did not take long for the sohei to become one of the most feared and least controllable forces in Japan. The monks were reputed to have magical powers that could perform miracles and inflict curses. They did not rely solely on magic, however. Their martial skills were awesome, particularly when they wielded the naginata, a long pole with a long, finely honed blade. Many an enemy head or limb was separated from its owner in one whirl of the naginata. They terrorized the government by placing spirit-containing shrines in Kyoto streets, and defying anyone to move it, on pain of incurring divine fury. One samurai who attempted to live up to the samurai reputation for bravery and ferocity actually shot an arrow into such a shrine. When the monks demanded severe retribution for the crime, however, the emperor, who knew that only his samurai stood between him and the sohei, imposed a symbolic fine on the offending samurai.

The sohei were involved in the Gempei war, and produced many heroes – Benkei among them. They suffered severe losses at the hand of Taira Shigihara, who proudly exhibited their impaled heads.

The end of the sohei era came in 1571, when the warlord, Oda Nobunaga, realized that political stability could never be achieved when the sohei were permitted to interfere in clan warfare. He deployed his troops around Mount Hiei, set fire to thousands of buildings, and killed any monks who attempted to escape the conflagration.

Nakano Kazuma Toshiaki

akano Kazuma Toshiaki presented an analogy between the use of old vessels in the Tea Ceremony and a retainer of low birth who rises in status because of his merits. He said that some people consider it uncouth to use old vessels for the Tea Ceremony, and it is preferable to use clean, new ones. Others think that old vessels should be used because new ones are too ostentatious. He claims that both are wrong, because the old vessels, used as they may be by the low-born people, are also used by the higher classes because of their value. The same is true of retainers who rise from their low-born status to the higher classes on of their own merits. It is wrong to think that a person from a low family cannot do the same work as a person from a high family, or that a simple foot soldier cannot become a leader. A person who has risen thanks to his own merits should be valued and respected more than a person who was born into the higher classes.

Hagakura

Sakanoue no Haruzumi's Humiliation

Sakanoue no Haruzumi was one of the Governor's armed men. He was a good warrior, but his career came to an ignominious end during a business trip to Kyoto.

He never traveled unarmed, because he knew that he had enemies in various places. On this particular trip, he was accompanied by armed guards in order to ensure his safety.

One night, he and his men were walking through the Kyoto streets when they came face to face with a group of nobles on horseback, preceded by an arrogant vanguard, who approached Haruzumi and his men and insisted that they dismount, lower their weapons, and lie down in the road. Powerless to object, Haruzumi and his men did as the vanguard ordered, and waited for the nobles to pass. Suddenly, they felt their faces being pushed into the dirt. Haruzumi struggled to look up, and to his astonishment, instead of seeing a group of nobles, he saw a band of mounted hooligans, fully armed and protected with armor. They aimed their bows and arrows at Haruzumi and threatened to kill him if he so much as breathed.

Haruzumi was beside himself with anger and frustration. He had been outwitted by a bunch of tough robbers, and if he wanted to live, he had to comply with their commands. The robbers roughly disrobed and disarmed them, and stole all of their weapons, shoes and clothing, saddles, and horses.

After the brigands had left, and Haruzumi and his men were sitting naked and shocked in the road, Haruzumi chastised himself for not having been more alert and attacking and killing the robbers. He could not forgive himself for having been taken in by the stratagem of the vanguard. The robbers had severely tricked and humiliated him, and he had no choice but to renounce his warrior status and demote himself to a mere side-runner.

Brave men

Unless a warrior is detached from life and death, he is useless. While the saying, "All abilities come from one mind" seems to concern conscious matters, it actually refers to detachment from life and death. Such detachment enables you to achieve anything. For this reason, the martial arts are connected to it, because they lead to the Way.

Brave men are ones who conduct themselves well when they die, and there are many such men. However, people who are habitually eloquent and articulate but cannot meet their deaths calmly are not considered to be brave.

In order to determine wind direction during battle, wind-bells are used. At night, fire can be lit in the direction of the wind, and the attack can be made from the opposite direction. Inform your allies of this strategy. Wind-bells are essential in order to determine the direction of the wind.

Hagakura

The Cool-Headed Fujiwara no Yasumasa

One night, a man called Hakamadare, the acknowledged king of the muggers, was on the prowl for some new clothes. He was a master of his profession, and there was no one who could match his strategies, skill and speed when relieving an unwitting victim of his possessions.

While he was reconnoitering locations that seemed to have potential as far as finding suitable clothing was concerned, he reached an isolated avenue (it was already late at night, and most people were at home). There he saw a very well-dressed man strolling along and playing the flute, with not a care in the world. Hakamadare had no trouble visualizing himself dressed in that elegant hunting robe, his legs nice and warm in the trouser-skirt that the victim would generously hand over to him.

Something in the man's bearing, however, deterred Hakamadare from simply running up to him, knocking him down, and tearing his clothes off. Unaccountably, the man scared him. He was not the usual sort of victim. Hakamadare kept his distance and followed the man down the avenue. The man seemed to be unaware of his presence, and played the flute with greater nonchalance than ever.

Hakamadare couldn't stand it anymore. It was time to scare the living daylights out of this flute-playing guy. He rushed up to him, making as much noise as he could, hoping that the man would freeze in terror and relinquish his clothes without a fuss. This was not to be, however. To Hakamadare's astonishment, the guy turned around, a quizzical look on his face, and continued his musical endeavors. Hakamadare was completely spooked. He turned tail and fled.

Frustrated, he repeated the maneuver several more times – with the same result. Who was this guy, for heaven's sake? By now, they had walked over half a mile down the avenue, and Hakamadare was thinking that this was ridiculous – he had to do something more drastic. Drawing his sword, he ran

menacingly up to the man. This time – finally – the man stood still, stopped playing the flute, turned to him with an inquiring expression, and asked: "What exactly do you think you're doing?"

Hakamadare thought his last hour had come. Struck dumb with fear, he threw himself onto the ground, trying to block out what was happening. What the hell was going on here? Was this dude a ghost or a devil or what? No one had ever humiliated super-mugger Hakamadare in this way before.

The man wouldn't let up. He repeated his question, and Hakamadare felt as if he was being interrogated by the supreme judge. He was compelled to answer, "Trying to mug you." He even told the man his name.

When the man heard Hakamadare's name, he nodded sagely and said that he had heard of him and his lethal cunning. He told Hakamadare to get up and follow him. To Hakamadare's astonishment, the guy started walking once more and resumed playing the flute. Hakamadare followed him as if hypnotized, his emotions a mixture of mystification, fright, and amazement. Was this just a flesh-and-blood man, or some really scary supernatural being?

After a while, they reached a large house. The man opened the gate, removed his shoes on the porch, and entered. Hakamadare realized that he must own the place. The man reappeared and beckoned to him. Hakamadare went over to the door, and the man offered him a handsome cotton outfit. He told Hakamadare, "Listen, man, if you ever need any clothing, just come and ask me. If you keep on attacking people like that, instead of just telling them what you want, someone will hurt you one day."

Stunned, Hakamadare walked away and thought about this weird experience. He suddenly realized that the house he had just visited belonged to the Governor of Settsu, Fujiwara no Yasumasa.

Hakamadare did not always get away with his crimes. He was occasionally arrested, and, when recounting the story of his encounter with Yasumasa, would remark about how peculiar and frightening the man was.

Tazaki Geki

T he warrior, Tazaki Geki, wore very ornate armor during the attack on the Shimabara castle, much to the disgust of Lord Katsushige. From then on, every time the latter saw something flashy, he compared it to Geki's armor.

The moral of this story is that ostentatious armor and military gear are perceived as being weak, since they reveal the wearer's heart.

S ome people who have little knowledge pretend that they know a great deal. This is because they are inexperienced. A person who really does have knowledge will not flaunt it. He is refined.

Hagakura

Taira no Munetsune: A Man of Few Words

One night, Fujiwara no Yorimichi, the Lord of Uji, wanted the monk, Myoson, to perform an errand for him at the fairly distant Mii Temple. He equipped the monk with a nice steady horse, and asked for a volunteer to accompany the monk on his mission. One of the Outer Palace Guards, Munetsune, immediately offered to do so, and Yorimichi instructed him to have the monk back by dawn.

Munetsune lived very frugally – he only had one manservant, had a spare pair of straw sandals, and kept his bow and arrows in the night duty room. When he had received his orders from Yorimichi, he tucked up his trouser-skirt and put on his sandals – ostensibly preparing for a long trip on foot – and slung his bow and arrows over his shoulder. He went over to where the monk was waiting for him on horseback. Myoson was amazed that Munetsune had no horse, but Munetsune assured him that this would not delay their journey in any way.

Munetsune's servant, holding a lamp, led the way, and when they had gone about half a mile, Myoson froze in terror: two armed men in black were approaching them. When they saw Munetsune, they knelt and indicated the horses they had brought for him and his servant. They had also brought him riding boots, which he put on over his sandals.

The monk felt much better now, with two mounted armed men accompanying him. However, a couple of hundred yards down the track, two similarly dressed and armed men on horseback came out of nowhere and, without a word, joined Munetsune's little group. The monk's astonishment increased by the second.

This procedure repeated itself every 200 yards or so until there was a retinue of about 30 men, traveling in silence. Myoson, totally intrigued by Munetsune's unusual actions, realized that they had reached the Mii Temple.

When he had done whatever errand he had been told to do, the group set out on the return journey. Now the procedure reversed itself, and soon pairs of men and horses disappeared silently into the darkness, until, by the time they reached Yorimichi's estate, there were only the original three of them – the monk, Munetsune (on foot and in his straw sandals), and the manservant (also on foot).

Myoson was overcome with curiosity and rushed off to report to Yorimichi, who was waiting for him. He told him about the errand he had done, and then made some remark about what an unusual guy Munetsune was – after all, he had quite a gang of armed men at his disposal.

Unfortunately for him, Yorimichi did not rise to the bait, and Myoson was left with nothing but unanswered questions.

Ghost warriors

Ruses during battle were accepted among the warrior samurai, especially when the army of one commander stormed the fortress of another commander. These ruses – particularly those that succeeded – were highly lauded, and their descriptions appeared in the battle reports. In order to penetrate the enemy fortresses, samurai would dress up as women or farmers and conceal their weapons inside musical instruments or farm implements. Alternatively, they would pretend to be dead in order to distract their foes and attack them.

One of the most famous ruses was the use of "ghost warriors" – or, in other words, scarecrows that resembled samurai. A commander by the name of Kusunoki perfected this trick in the 14th century, while defending his fortress against attack by Hojo warriors who outnumbered his own forces. He ordered the preparation of scores of scarecrows dressed in samurai armor and bearing weapons, and placed them around the gate of the fortress. He stationed his archers on the wall. When the massive Hojo forces attacked the fortress, the archers shot arrows over the wall relentlessly. The Hojo samurai pushed forward, intent upon hand-to-hand combat with the enemy samurai, thus attaining glory (in the knowledge that the moment they were up close to the enemy samurai, the shower of arrows would cease). However, when they reached the gate and surrounded the "samurai," and before they had the chance to discover that they were faced with scarecrows, hundreds of heavy stones pelted down on them from the walls and pailfuls of boiling water were poured onto them. Some

thousand Hojo samurai warriors were killed or injured in the battle at the gate, and the bravest of them, who survived the arrows, stones, and boiling water, discovered that their glory was based on nothing but the slaying of magnificently dressed scarecrows!

Yoshitsune's Letter

After Minamoto Yoshitsune defeated the Taira, he attempted to meet up with his brother, Yoritomo, in Kamakura, but Yoritomo decided that he should cool his heels for three weeks in a nearby village. Deeply insulted by his brother's snub, Yoshitsune wrote a letter to one of Yoritomo's ministers, complaining that instead of being commended for his victory over the Taira, he was being slandered, accused, and ostracized –

and worst of all, his achievements were being ignored. He went on to describe the incredible hardships he had suffered on the battlefield, and how he had appealed to all the gods and invoked all the spirits to help him refute the accusations of harmful ambition and pledge his loyalty to his lord. All his efforts had been futile.

Not only did Yoritomo ostracize his brother, but he sent warriors to eliminate him. Yoshitsune escaped with his loyal retainer, Benkei, and his pregnant mistress, Shizuka. They wandered around, seeking shelter. At a certain point, Shizuka could no longer suffer the hardships of the journey, and she was left behind. One of Yorimoto's followers captured her, but she refused to divulge any information. Forced to entertain Yorimoto, she sang a love song to Yoshitsune, which enraged Yorimoto. Fortunately for her,

Yorimoto's wife intervened, and her life was spared. Her infant son was less fortunate, however – Yorimoto was not about to repeat Taira's mistake of letting a potential avenger live.

Meanwhile, Yoshitsune and his few followers found shelter with the lord of Mutsu. This respite was short-lived: after the lord's death in 1189, his son, Fujiwara Yasuhira, attacked Yoshitsune and his men in an attempt to please Yorimoto. A fierce battle ensued, leaving only Benkei and one other warrior to defend Yoshitsune, who was meditating at the back of the house. Soon only Benkei was left, and, arrows piercing every corner of his armor, he raced toward the enemy. They were dumbfounded, and did not dare go up to him. He stood his ground until one of the enemy samurai approached him and discovered that he was dead.

At this point, Yoshitsune realized that the game was over, and he killed his family and then committed seppuku. Yasuhira sent his head to Yorimoto, but his action backfired when the latter sent troops to confiscate the vast and valuable Mutsu lands. Now it was Yasuhira's head that was taken to Yorimoto by one of Yasuhira's followers. The follower, who expected to be rewarded for his loyalty to Yorimoto, was beheaded in order to serve as an example to Yorimoto's samurai of what they could expect for betraying their lord. With this strategy, Yorimoto added 50,000 mounted archers to his army, and was now free to establish his rule in Kamakura.

As for Yoshitsune, he became the subject of myths and legends, some of which even credited him with having escaped to mainland Asia and emerging as Genghis Khan.

One of Lord Mitsushige's pageboys

O ne of Lord Mitsushige's pageboys, Tomoda Shozaemon, fell in love with a leading actor. His infatuation led him to squander all his means – money, clothes, furniture – until he was compelled to steal a valuable sword, which he entrusted to a spearman to take to a pawn shop.

The spearman denounced him, however, and both he and the spearman were sentenced to death by Mitsushige, after the investigator, Yamamoto Gorozaemon, stated the facts of the case. Gorozaemon came and told the pageboy to prepare for his death, and the pageboy accepted his fate bravely. Instead of the assistant who was supposed to attend the pageboy's seppuku and deal the decapitating death blow, another assistant, a foot soldier, was sneaked in from the side in order to decapitate him.

The pageboy was very calm when he greeted the man whom he believed to be his assistant. However, when the foot soldier suddenly appeared, sword drawn, ready to decapitate him, he jumped up and protested vigorously that he would never allow him to decapitate him. That was the end of his dignified behavior, and he displayed great cowardice. He was eventually pinned down and executed.

The investigator later said that the pageboy would probably have faced death valiantly if he hadn't been tricked.

Hagakura

The Tragic Love of Two Enemies

The Lord of the province of Etjigo instructed his chief minister to order one of the pages, Senpatji, to kill the samurai Shingokei for reasons that were unknown to the minister. Although Senpatji trusted the minister implicitly, the significance and weight of the order were such that he felt he needed the reassurance of the Lord himself that this was in fact what he was expected to do.

The Lord confirmed the minister's message. Senpatji was devastated about what he had to do, because Shingokei was one of his best friends. However, an order from the Lord could not be ignored, so off he went to Shingokei's house, where he told him that this is what he had been instructed to do, and killed his friend. When Shingokei's servants tried to detain him, he explained that he had been acting on his Lord's orders.

The Lord not only deprived Shingokei's wife of her husband – he confiscated everything and reduced her to dire poverty. She was grief-stricken at the death of her beloved husband – they had only been married a year –

and would have committed suicide had it not been for the fact that she was pregnant. She left Etjigo and, after a long and difficult journey, reached an outlying province, where she settled in a village and eked out a living by doing needlework. Her only possessions were a pair of swords and a harp, which she would play when loneliness and sorrow overcame her.

Shortly afterwards, she gave birth alone, and took care of her child with love and devotion. She noticed his resemblance to her beloved husband both in his looks and in his refined behavior. When the boy, Shynosuke, was 14, Senpatji, his father's killer, arrived in the village. He had been expelled from the Lord's court for some misdemeanor, and had settled in a nearby town. During a hunting trip with a friend, Senpatji came across the widow's hut and heard beautiful music emanating from it. The men stopped and peeked in. They saw a lovely woman in her mid-30s playing the harp, with her son, a gorgeous young boy, sitting next to her and practicing writing. It was clear that they were of noble birth, and for the life of him, Senpatji couldn't understand what she was doing in this God-forsaken place.

Senpatji and his friend knocked on the

door and entered the hut. After apologizing for disturbing the woman and her son, they went on their way. Senpatji could not forget the beautiful boy, however. He was so taken by him that he returned to the hut and befriended the little family. He and the boy fell deeply in love, and finally he took both the mother and son to his town and set them up in his home. They spent a tranquil year living like this.

One day, the widow realized that Senpatji closely resembled her husband's killer. After asking him some leading questions, she realized that her and her son's patron was in fact the man who had caused her to become a penniless, forlorn widow. She explained this to Shynosuke, and told him that it was his obligation to avenge his father's death by killing Senpatji. The youth was astounded, and tried to convince his mother that Senpatji had not killed his father out of personal malice. He had been given an order that he could not refuse. If anything, the Lord should be killed. Shynosuke attempted to appeal to his mother's gratitude to Senpatji for his goodness to them – to no avail, however. She was furious, and accused Shynosuke of cowardice and of dishonoring a samurai. She claimed that she would never have accepted Senpatji's assistance and his affection for her son had she realized who he was. If Shynosuke was not prepared to do the deed, she would do it herself. So saying, she grabbed one of the swords.

Shynosuke stopped her, told her to calm down, and assured her that he would kill Senpatji. His mind was in turmoil. He had to kill the man he had loved for two years; however, he would not do so without explaining his reasons.

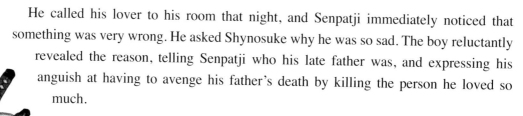

He called his lover to his room that night, and Senpatji immediately noticed that something was very wrong. He asked Shynosuke why he was so sad. The boy reluctantly revealed the reason, telling Senpatji who his late father was, and expressing his anguish at having to avenge his father's death by killing the person he loved so much.

Senpatji did not attempt to prevaricate. He admitted that he had been ordered to kill Shynosuke's father, and added that he would gladly die at the boy's hands. So saying, he discarded his weapons and bared his neck to Shynosuke's sword. The youth insisted that he could not kill his lover in cold blood, and wanted to engage in a sword-fight.

His mother, who had witnessed the whole scene, called Shynosuke and told her that she admired both him and Senpatji. She permitted them to spend one last night together – but the next day, Shynosuke was to kill him.

The lovers drank wine and spent their last night together. In the morning, Shynosuke's mother entered the room and saw that they were still sleeping. She tried to rouse Shynosuke, but he did not respond. When she drew back the blanket, she saw that he had pierced both of their hearts with his sword. Devastated, the mother killed herself in the same room.

A young man

A young man who came down with smallpox insisted on joining the forces that were attacking the castle in the province of Hizen. Despite his parents' protests, he was adamant about going. He told them that he would be happy to die on the way, since his master had been good to him, and it was not for him to decide that he would not be of any use while he was ill.

During his tour of duty at the front, the weather was bitterly cold, but the young man ignored his state of health, and was not too fastidious about his personal hygiene, either. He did not add layers of clothing, nor did he remove his armor. Although he ignored the dictates of cleanliness, he recovered fully and fought to the death for his master. This shows that a lack of hygiene should not automatically be condemned.

Upon hearing the story of the young man, the teacher, Suzuki Shozo, stated that the young man would be protected by the gods in heaven for what he had done. Throwing away his life for his master was a cleansing act. The young man did not need death by smallpox when he could opt to give his life for a just cause.

Hagakura

I n Japan, the Kendo or "Way of the Sword" was synonymous with nobility. Ever since the Samurai class arose in the 900's, knowledge of the military arts was considered the highest form of learnedness. Study of the Kendo was inspired by the spirit of Shinto and infused with the Zen principles. The first schools of Kendo were established in the fourteenth century and continue to exist to this very day.

Musashi lived during a period when the samurai were thought of as the elite of society. In reality however, they had no means of support other than ownership of castles or land, if they had such. Many of the samurai during this time were forced to abandon their swords and become artisans. Others, like Musashi, continued along the path of the Kendo, searching for the "warrior's ideal".

Miyamoto Musashi is the commonly accepted name of Shinmen Musashi No Kami Fujiwara No Genshin. He was born in 1584 in Miyamoto, in the province of Mimasaka. Musashi was orphaned at a young age, and was educated in the home of his uncle, a priest. A large and aggressive youth, he possessed a very strong will. When only thirteen, he succeeded in slaying a man in single combat.

At age sixteen, after another victory in battle, Musashi left home and wandered from place to place, competing in many battles in order to prove his proficiency as a warrior. He lived a nomadic life, never marrying, moving across the reaches of Japan in the coldest days of winter wearing scant protection from the elements, and allowing his hair to grow wild. It is told that he never bathed for fear of leaving his weapon unattended, and thus he was quite vulgar and repulsive in appearance.

Musashi's most famous battle took place in the year 1612 in Ogura, in the province of Bunzen, against Sasaki Kojiro, a notorious young fighter. As the two stood face to face and Kojiro drew his long sword, Musashi called out to him, "You will not need that any longer!" When Kojiro advanced, Musashi went toward him, keeping his own sword still at his side. As his opponent made the first cut, Musashi came down on him from above directly onto his

head using a boat oar. Many say that after this act, Musashi threw down the oar, and brandishing both of his swords over the body of his dead opponent, shouted in victory. After this battle, Musashi never again used a real sword in battle. His was unbeatable, and from that time forward, he devoted himself entirely to understanding the way of the Kendo.

As Musashi himself bears witness in his writings, he achieved enlightened understanding of strategy in 1634, at the age of fifty-one, following many battles and six actual wars. During that year, he settled in Ogura, along with his adopted son, Iori, and from then until his death he never left the Island of Kyushu.

After spending six years in Ogura, Musashi was invited to sojourn as a guest in the castle of the lord of Kumamoto. There he taught the military arts, and created ink drawings which are to this day the most famous of their kind in Japan.

In 1643, Musashi retired from society and secluded himself in a cave. It was here that he composed the book Go Rin No Sho, The Book of Five Rings, which he dedicated to his student Teruo. Musashi died just a few days after completing the writing of the book.

Musashi was known in Japan as the Saint of the Sword. And his book, Gorin No Sho, **"The Book of Five Rings"** was mandatory Kendo reading. The book was meant to be, according to Musashi himself, a "guide for a person wishing to learn strategy".

Musashi wrote another book called The 35 Articles on the Art of Swordsmanship, which was commissioned by the head of the Hosokawa clan. This book describes the physical and psychological aspects of combat. Musashi elaborates upon where the warrior should look during the duel, how his eyes should be focused, and on what his mind should concentrate. His main message is that the eyes should be able to see the opponent in his physical entirety in order to parry any kind of blow, but they should also look deep into his mind and character in order to understand where his opponent is coming from. The main point is not to allow the opponent to breach the privacy of the warrior's mind through his eyes.

For many years, I have trained in the Way of Strategy which is called Ni Ten Ichi Ryu. For the first time, I shall now put an explanation of it into writing. I am writing during the first ten days of the tenth month of the twentieth year of Kanei. [1645] I have ascended mount Iwato in Kiyusho to extol heaven, to pray to Kwannon, and to go down on bended knee before Buddha. I am a warrior from the province of Harima. I am Shinmen Musashi No Kami Fujiwara No Genshin. I am sixty years of age.

Even in my youth, my heart was captured by the Way of Strategy. My first duel took place when I was thirteen years of age. I beat down a strategist from the Shinto School – Arima Kihei. At age thirteen I struck down the talented strategist Tadashima Akiyama. When I was twenty-one years of age, I went up to the capital and fought many strategists of different origins. I never lost even a single contest.

Afterwards, I went from province to province, dueling with strategists from varying schools. Victory was always mine, even when I faced as many as sixty opponents. This took place when I was between the ages of thirteen and twenty eight.

When I reached the age of thirty, I looked over my past. My victories previously were not on account of my having mastered strategy. It may have been on account of my natural talent, or perhaps my victories were ordained by heaven, or perhaps the other schools' strategies were weak. Following this, I studied morning until evening, trying to find the principle, until at age fifty I finally came upon the realization of the Way of Strategy.

Since that time I have lived without following any particular doctrine. With the help of strategy, I have practiced my many skills and talents, without the benefit of any teacher. I did not use the law of Buddha or the teachings of Confucius to write this book. Nor did I use any books or chronicles on military tactics. I take quill in hand in order to explain the true spirit of the Ichi School as it is reflected in the Way of heaven and Kwannon. It is now the evening of the tenth day of the tenth month, the hour of the tiger.

Miyamoto Musashi

The Book of Five Rings
The Water Book

● The Five Approaches ●

●**The First Approach:** Assume the Middle Stance. Encounter your opponent with the point of your sword aimed right at his face. When you make contact with your opponent and he attacks, deflect his sword to the right. Next, hit downwards, so that his sword returns upward, and keep your sword in the downward position. When he attacks again, strike at the enemy's arms from below.

The five approaches must be learned through repeated training with the sword. When these are mastered, you will be able to offset every attack of the enemy. There is none other than these five approaches, and they must be practiced.

●**The Second Approach:** Assume the Upper Stance and attack the enemy at the exact moment that he strikes out at you. Should you miss, hold the position of your sword as is, and strike again by bringing it upwards as the opponent attacks again. This same strike can then be repeated.

The approaches can be taken with variations in mood and timing. With continuous training you will understand them and you will always win using the ways of the sword. Practice faithfully.

●**The Third Approach:** Assume the Lower Stance. Be ready to attack your opponent from below. When the enemy advances, strike upward at his hands. Your opponent may then try to dash your sword down. If so, let his strike pass by, and then cut his upper arm. Staying in the lower attitude, you attack the moment at the same moment that he strikes out.

The lower stance is appropriate for beginners and more advanced, and should be practiced often with the long sword.

●**The Fourth Approach:** Assume the Left Side Stance. Hit your opponent's hands from below, as he attacks. As he moves to deflect your strike, concentrate on hitting his hands, and parry the path of his sword. Cut crosswise from above your shoulder.

This is the Way of the Sword. It is a way to defeat your opponent by parrying the path of his attack. You should carefully study this.

●**The Fifth Approach:** Assume the Right Side Stance with your sword to your right. As your enemy approaches, move your sword from the lower side, to the upper position. Then immediately slash straight downward.

This approach will facilitate your knowing the Way of the Sword well. If you practice this method you will be able to deftly handle a heavy long sword.

I have not written about these five approaches in detail. You must come to know my style and general rhythm and harmony in order to anticipate the opponent's sword's direction. To be practiced in the five approaches, you must train in them daily. By seriously understanding these five approaches, you will be assured of victory by discerning your opponent's intent. This must be considered carefully.

Whichever your stance may be, do not focus your attention on the matter of the stance. Concentrate only on the cut. The stance should be high or low in accordance with the situation. The upper, lower, and middle stances are decisive. The right and left side stances are flowing. The left and right side stances must be used when there is an obstacle above the head or to one side. The decision to use left or right depends on the location of the obstacle.

The essence of the Way is: in order to understand the principle of the stance, you must grasp well the middle stance. The middle stance is the heart. If we look at wide reaching strategy, the middle stance is the commander, and the four others follow the commander. This should be appreciated.

● The Way of the Long Sword[1] ●

Knowing the Way of the Long Sword entails knowing how to wield the sword with two fingers, rather than carrying it in the usual manner. If we are well aware of the path of the sword, we are able to handle it with ease.

If you try to wield the long sword quickly, you will be mistaken in the Way. In order to control the long sword efficiently, you must maintain calmness. If you try to wield it speedily, as you would a fan, or a short sword, you will find yourself using by mistake, "short-sword chopping". You will not be able to cut a person with the long sword using this method.

*1. **the Way of the Long Sword:** the way as a way of life, and as the way of the cut of a sword's blade. According to Kendo ethics, the sword has a natural movement, which is connected to natural behavior.*

● Stance-No-Stance Instructions ●

Stance-No-Stance means that there is no need for what are referred to as the stances of the long sword. However there do exist five ways of holding the long sword. The way you hold your sword must be that which makes it easiest for you to cut the enemy well, taking into account your situation and location relative to the enemy. When your energy dips, you can switch from the upper to the middle stance and from there, lift the sword slightly and move back to the upper stance. From the lower stance you can lift up slightly and move to the middle stance as the need calls for it. Depending on the situation, either of the two side stances can become middle stance or lower stance by moving a bit toward the center.

The most important principle when taking a sword into your hands is to cut down your enemy, whatever means need be applied to this end. Whether you parry, strike, hit, hold or touch your enemy's cutting sword, you must cut the enemy in the same motion. This is essential. If you think only of hitting, holding, springing at, or striking the enemy, this will not be sufficient to cut him down. You must think in first and foremost about performing the motion which will bring about cutting him. You must study this matter thoroughly.

Strategic stance, on a wider scale, is called "battle array". These stances are the keys to victory in battle. Using inflexible formations is undesirable. Learn this well.

• To Hit the Enemy in One Count •

The significance of "one count" is that when you have closed in on the enemy, you hit him as swiftly and directly as you can, without moving your body or changing your mind, so as not to give the enemy time to consider his next moves. Timing the hitting of the enemy before he can decide to withdraw, break, or hit, is called "one count".

You must practice in order to achieve this timing, so that you will be able to attack instantaneously.

• Two Count Timing •

When you quickly hit your opponent, and he retreats only to tense for a further attack, you must feint a slash. And then, then he relaxes, chase after him and hit him. This is the "two count timing".

It is difficult to achieve this simply by reading this book, but with the help of several lessons you will come to understand it.

• No Plan – No Concept[1] •

With this method, when the enemy strikes and you also decide to strike, you hit with your body, and with your spirit, and your hands strike out of a void, emerging instantaneously. This is the no plan – no concept strike.

It is a very effective method of hitting and is often used. You must practice it well in order to understand it.

*1. **No Plan - No Concept:** this is the ability to act naturally and calmly in the face of danger. It is perfect harmony with the universe.*

● Running Water Strike ●

The running water strike is used when fighting an enemy blade to blade. When he tires and retreats quickly, and tries to hit you with his sword, you must expand your body and your spirit, and cut him as slowly as possible with your long sword, using your power as that of water from a flowing stream. You will certainly be able to cut if you master this. You must discern your enemy's advantage.

● Continuous Cut ●

When you and the enemy attack simultaneously, and your swords meet, hit his head, hand, and feet, all in one motion. When you cut in several places with one sword stroke, this is called the continuous cut. You must practice this. It is used with great frequency. You must put it into practice until you are able to understand it.

● Fire and Stone Cut ●

The fire and stone cut is used when your sword and the enemy's cross, and you cut as strongly as possible without raising your sword even the slightest bit. Cut quickly and strongly with your hands, body, and legs. If you practice well you will be able to cut with great force.

● Red Leaf Cut[1] ●

The red leaf cut is knocking the enemy's sword to the ground and taking control of it for yourself. When the enemy stands before you intent on striking, hitting or parrying, you must strongly strike at the enemy's long sword using the No Plan No Concept perhaps, or the Fire and Stone Cut. Keep beating down his sword without letting up, until he is forced to drop it to the ground.

If you train this way it will become easy for you to cause the enemy to relinquish his sword. You must practice this over and over.

*1. **The red leaf cut:** Musashi probably means the leaves falling from the tree.*

● The Body in Place of the Long Sword ●

This can also be called the long sword in place of the body. Usually we move the body and sword with synchronization in order to cut the enemy. However, in accordance with the system of cutting which the enemy is using, you can attack him first with your body, and cut him afterwards with your sword. If it is not possible to move his body, you can first cut with the long sword, but generally you should hit first with your body and then cut with the sword. You must investigate this well and practice this type of hit.

● The Cut and the Slash ●

The cut and the slash are distinct one from the other. The cut is decisive, and done with a brave spirit. The slash is simply a touching of the enemy. Even if the slash is a strong one and the enemy dies, it is still a slash. With you cut, the spirit is resolute and set. You must understand this. If at first you slash the hand or foot of your opponent, you must afterward strongly cut him. Slashing is similar to touching. When you come to realize this, they become recognizable. Study this thoroughly.

● The Body of the Chinese Monkey[1] ●

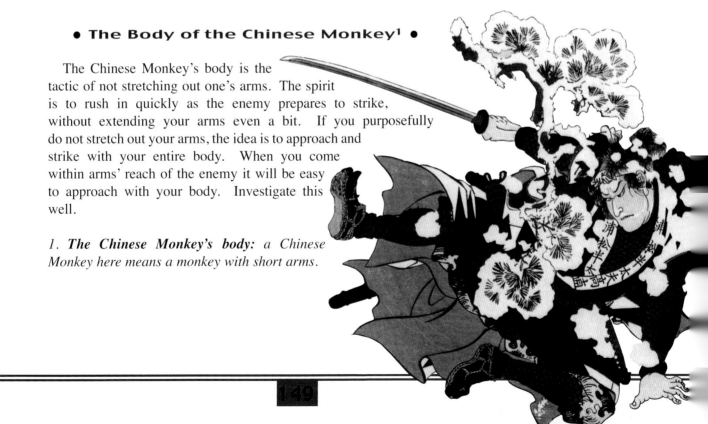

The Chinese Monkey's body is the tactic of not stretching out one's arms. The spirit is to rush in quickly as the enemy prepares to strike, without extending your arms even a bit. If you purposefully do not stretch out your arms, the idea is to approach and strike with your entire body. When you come within arms' reach of the enemy it will be easy to approach with your body. Investigate this well.

*1. **The Chinese Monkey's body:** a Chinese Monkey here means a monkey with short arms.*

● The Glue and Lacquer Body[1] ●

The essence of the glue and lacquer tactic is to come close to your enemy's body, and to effectively stick to him. When you approach the enemy, attach yourself firmly to his head, his body, and his legs. There is a tendency to stick only to the head or feet but to leave out the rest of the body. There is a tendency to stick only to the head or feet but to leave out the rest of the body. You should stick firmly leaving no space between your body and the enemy's. Think this over carefully.

*1. **The body of the glue and lacquer:** a Japanese tradition of coating furniture, tools, weapons, and armor.*

● Contest of Height ●

The contest of height means that when you are in proximity to the enemy you must strive to maintain the height advantage, with no letup. Extend your legs, stretch your hips, and stretch your neck, keeping your face aligned with his, intent on winning, and on being taller. When you feel you have the height advantage, hold strongly to it. You must make great effort to learn this.

● Applying Glue ●

When you and your enemy strike simultaneously, you must attach your sword to his with stickiness, and hold your swords together so that they do not separate, and you absorb his blow. The spirit of the application of glue is not to hit out with great strength. Rather the point is to make it impossible for the swords to separate easily. Do this as calmly as you can, while adhering strongly to the enemy's sword. The difference between "stickiness" and "entanglement" is that stickiness is steadfast and entanglement is weak. This must be appreciated.

● The Body Strike ●

The body strike is delivered when the enemy lets down his guard momentarily. Turn your face slightly sideways, and strike at the enemy's chest, while thrusting your left shoulder outwards. Come toward the opponent with the intention of repelling him, and strike as mightily as possible, in rhythm with your breathing. If you succeed with this method of closing in on the enemy, you be able to throw him back a distance of ten or twenty feet. You can strike a fatal blow in this manner. Practice faithfully.

● Three Ways to Parry the Enemy's Attack ●

There are three ways to parry an attack.

Push the enemy's sword to your right, as if toward his eyes, as he attacks.

Or

Thrust the enemy's sword toward his right eye, as if snapping his neck.

Or

When you have a short sword, move in quickly towards the enemy and hit his face with your left hand.

These are the three methods of parrying. Always keep in mind that you can use your left fist to punch at the enemy's face. It is necessary to practice hard for this.

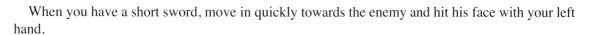

● Stabbing the Face

●

Stabbing the face means that when you are in confrontation with the enemy you set your spirit with the intention of stabbing your sword into his face, with the tip of your long sword following the line of the blades. If you remain intent on stabbing your long sword into his face, his face and body will be pulled into control. Once the enemy is under control, you will have several opportunities to beat him. You must concentrate on this. When during the battle, the enemy's body becomes controllable, you can quickly be victorious, and so you mustn't forget to stab the sword into his face. You should acquire this important skill through practice.

● Stabbing the Heart ●

When during a fight there are obstacles above or to the sides, making it difficult to cut, you must thrust at your opponent. You must stab your long sword into the breast of the enemy without letting the point of your sword waver, with the blade of the sword before the enemy's eyes, with the intent to deflect his long sword sideways. This principle is very efficient should you become tired or for some other reason your long sword has difficulty cutting. You should understand the use of this method.

● Scolding "Tut–Tut" ●

When the enemy tries to counter attack just as you attack, you again counter attack from below, and try to hold him down. You cut with a quick rhythm, scolding the enemy. As you thrust up, yell "tut!" and cut. Yell "tut!" again. The timing for this cut is used repeatedly in exchanges of blows. The scolding "tut-tut" should be used making the cut at the same moment that you raise your sword as if to thrust at the enemy. You must learn this well by training repeatedly.

● The Slapping Parry ●

The smacking parry is carried out when you are up against the enemy and you absorb his attacking cut with your long sword with a "tee-dum, tee-dum" rhythm, while slapping at his sword, and cutting him.

The spirit of the slapping parry is not simply slapping fiercely or parrying, but slapping the enemy's sword in accordance to his attack, when your intent is first and foremost to cut him quickly. If you understand the timing of the slapping, even during the most difficult of sword battles, the blade of your sword will not be repelled, even slightly. You must study this enough to understand.

● There are Many Enemies ●

The "many enemies" method is put into practice when you are fighting one against many. Draw your sword and also its accompanying sword, and use the right and left stances. The idea is to go after the enemies from side to side, even though they may come from all four directions. Pay attention to the order of their attacks, and counter first those who attack first. Take in your surroundings well, and make note of the attacking order, and cut right and left alternatively, with two swords. Waiting is not desirable. Always return quickly to the two side stances, cut the enemy as he advances, and repel them to the direction from which they start to attack. Whatever you may do, you must crash the enemy together, as if you were tying a line of fishes, and when it seems they are piled together, cut them fiercely, giving them no room to move.

● The Advantage When Exchanging Blows ●

You can learn to win by using the strategy of the long sword, but to explain it clearly in writing is not possible. You must train industriously in order to know how to be victorious.

According to the oral tradition, "The true way of strategy is revealed by the long sword".

● One Cut ●

You will be able to win using the "one cut". It will be hard to achieve this without learning strategy thoroughly. If you practice well in this way, strategy will flow from your mind and you will have the ability to win according to your will of mind. You should practice thoroughly.

● Direct Communication ●

The spirit of direct communication has been transmitted as the true way of the two swords. According to oral tradition, you must train thoroughly and make it part of your body.

Written in the NiTo Ichi School is the way of Ichi school sword fighting. In order to learn to win using the long sword strategically, first you must learn the five stances and the five approaches, and to incorporate the way of the long sword into your body. You must be in harmony with intent and rhythm, and wield your sword with natural movements of your body and legs, as they work together harmoniously with your mind. Being able to beat one enemy or two, will depend on your knowledge, right and wrong, of the martial arts.

Study what is in this book, one line at a time, and practice with opponents, until you grasp fully the principle of the Way.

Patiently and deliberately, learn the value of all of this, taking part in combat occasionally. Know your enemy's mind, whoever he may be.

You make a journey of a thousand miles by taking step after step.

With study and over time, you will achieve the spirit of a warrior. You will surpass today what you accomplished yesterday, and tomorrow you will go further still, until you will be able to vanquish more highly skilled men. Train according to this book, and don't allow your mind to get off the track.

No matter what opponent you may manage to defeat, it will not be the true Way if you do not do it according to these teachings.

If you retain these principles in mind, you will know how to beat even tens of opponents. You need also a strong knowledge of swordsmanship, so mind that you allow yourself many practice battles and duels.

It is the second year of Shoho, the twelfth day of the fifth month (1645)

ERRATA

ACKNOWLEDGMENTS. p. 6: The name of Germain Seligman should be added to the list of persons who generously helped in locating pictures and who extended many other courtesies.

TEXT: p. 26, line 11, *for* landscape *read* landscapes

CAPTIONS: p. 29, for *Varoquez* read *Varocquez*
           p. 92, line 36, for *Children Playing*
             read *Children's Game*
           p. 93, line 6, *omit* 100

Frontispiece: *Self Portrait*. 1892. Oil on board, 14 x 11″. Collection Mr. and Mrs. Sidney F. Brody, Los Angeles

2

Edouard Vuillard

by Andrew Carnduff Ritchie

The Museum of Modern Art, New York

in collaboration with

The Cleveland Museum of Art

Reprint Edition, 1969

Published for The Museum of Modern Art by Arno Press

Copyright 1954. The Museum of Modern Art, New York
Printed in the United States of America
Library of Congress card number: 54-6136

Reprint Edition, 1969   Arno Press
Library of Congress Catalog Card No. 79-86445

Contents

Acknowledgments

On behalf of the Trustees of the Museum of Modern Art and the Cleveland Museum of Art, I wish to extend grateful acknowledgment to Claude Roger-Marx, André Chastel and Jacques Salomon, the three French writers who have done most in recent years to estimate and to reveal Vuillard's contribution to the art of our time. Without their researches and their accounts growing out of personal contacts with the artist, this study could not have been made. Each of them has generously assisted me in a number of ways.

I am grateful also to William S. Lieberman for his excellent notes on Vuillard as a printmaker; to Miss Alice Bacon, Miss Ellen Mary Jones and Miss Alicia Legg, of the Department of Painting and Sculpture, for assistance in research and in translations of quoted material; to Alfred H. Barr, Jr., Monroe Wheeler and Miss Margaret Miller for reading my manuscript and making a number of valuable suggestions; to Mme Jacqueline Bouchot-Saupique, Louis Carré, Ralph F. Colin, Philip James, M. Knoedler & Co., Jacques Lindon, Helmut Lütjen, Porter McCray, William M. Milliken, Mlle Marcel Minet, Frank Perls, John Rewald, J. Rodrigues-Henriques, Paul Rosenberg, Siegfried Rosengart, Sam Salz, Miss Darthea Speyer, Mme H. O. Van der Wal, Daniel Wildenstein, Miss Lelia Wittler and Charles Zadok for help in locating pictures and for many other courtesies; and to the many museum directors in this country and abroad who took time to answer a question regarding Vuillards in their vicinity.

Above all, I am indebted to Hanna Fund, Cleveland, Ohio, and to the lenders to the exhibition. Their generous cooperation has made possible the first extensive showing of Vuillard's paintings and prints in this country.

ANDREW CARNDUFF RITCHIE

Edouard Vuillard

Edouard Vuillard was a strangely complex personality. Many of the secrets of his life will be revealed in 1980 when, by his will, his private journal can be made public. Until then we must depend on the accounts of his friends and the evidence of his art for whatever estimates we may make of him. His origins were petty bourgeois and, despite his later associations with a somewhat fashionable set in Parisian society, he remained in all essentials a petty bourgeois to his death. He was a retiring, silent, even timid little man, given only occasionally to bursts of anger. He suffered from a kind of melancholy or ennui, which he endured patiently. He was a great reader on art and was devoted to the poetry of Mallarmé; he read Paul Valéry, Jean Giraudoux and all of Baudelaire.[1] Devoutly religious in his youth, he retained throughout his life something of the Jansenist Catholic's respect for the homely Christian virtues of simplicity, sobriety and honesty. Yet he was not a puritan. He enjoyed good living and, while he remained a bachelor all his life, it is rumored that he had several love affairs. But, as became his upbringing, he seems never to have allowed passion of any kind to get out of hand. Nothing, apparently, was permitted to disturb the even course of the ménage he kept with his mother until her death in 1928.

His quiet, introspective nature was respected and admired by all his friends. He was a listener rather than a talker and, perhaps because he preferred to paint rather than to theorize about painting, he retained the friendship of everyone in his circle. But however inarticulate he may have appeared at artist discussions, he clearly had a mind of his own. Maurice Denis, one of his boyhood friends, wrote in 1898 to Vuillard from Rome and said, among other things: "The value of a work of art lies in the plenitude of the artist's effort, in the force of his will." Vuillard's answer is a better characterization of himself than perhaps any critic or fellow painter has given us. He replied: "I suffer too much in my life and my work from what you speak of, not to reply immediately ... It is not while I am working that I think of the technique of picture making or of immediate satisfaction. To speak generally—it is not while I am doing this or that, that I consider the quality of my actions (you have only to think of my diffidence and my character). Whatever I have the happiness to be working at, it is because there is an idea in me in which I have faith. As to the quality of the result, I do not worry myself ... I conceive, but in fact I actually experience only very rarely, that will and effort of which you like to speak. You have so

1 Thadée Natanson. *Peints à leur tour*, Albin Michel, Paris, 1948, p. 377.

long been accustomed by nature, education and circumstances and in presence of certain results that please you, to give a particular sense to the word *will* that you attempt to explain others, me for instance, by your own logic. You may sometimes deceive yourself. The important thing is that I have faith enough to produce. And I admit one could call that work. In general, I have a horror or rather a blue funk of general ideas which I haven't discovered for myself, but I don't deny their value. I prefer to be humble rather than pretend to understanding."[1]

Vuillard achieved an almost instantaneous success as a young painter in the '90s. After about 1905, however, for various reasons, his art began to attract less and less critical appreciation and by 1914 he withdrew almost completely from public exhibitions. It was not until 1936 that a considerable number of his early paintings was placed on exhibition and even so the occasion was an historical rather than a contemporary one—a review of the artists with whom he had been associated in his youth. In 1938, two years before his death, he was rather unwillingly induced to supervise the selection of a large retrospective exhibition of his work held at the Musée des Arts Décoratifs, and here many saw for the first time the full extent of his art and, particularly, the series of large decorative panels which had been hidden away in private houses. Since this exhibition, and especially since the last war, there has been a significant revival of interest in him. The 1938 exhibition undoubtedly inspired some of this interest. More important, perhaps, a revival of interest between the wars in the symbolist movement coincided with the revelation of Vuillard's distinctive contribution to it.

Vuillard was born in 1868 in Cuiseaux, Saône-et-Loire, the youngest child of a family of three. His father, a retired military officer, died in 1883, when Vuillard was fifteen. The family, meanwhile, had moved to Paris. His mother, a native of Paris, and twenty-seven years younger than her husband, decided on his death to occupy herself and support her family by going into business as a dressmaker. Her love and knowledge of the materials of her craft, which she was to transmit to her artist son, she must have come by directly. Her father and brother were both textile designers. Her workshop, where she employed two assistants, was first on the rue Daunou, and later in a room of the family apartment, on the ground floor of a house on the rue du Marché-Saint-Honoré.[2]

Vuillard's first school was one run by a Catholic teaching order, the Marist Brothers. He next attended the Ecole Rocroy and finally the Lycée Condorcet. It was the family intention to have him follow his father into the army by pre-

1 Quoted by Claude Roger-Marx. *Vuillard*, Editions de la Maison Française, New York, 1946, p. 20.
2 Vuillard and his mother remained at this apartment until 1896. They then moved to the rue Truffaut, in the Batignolles quarter, and afterwards to the rue de la Tour, near the Trocadero. Finally, after 1908, they moved to a house on the Square Vintimille. All of these addresses, it will be noted, are in a fairly restricted orbit and all are in quiet, middle-class districts.

paring him for the army college at St. Cyr. But his friends, and possibly the teaching at the Lycée Condorcet, decided him on an artist's course. Mallarmé taught English there until 1884, and it is of interest to note that Marcel Proust a few years later attended the same school. Vuillard's immediate school friends were Ker-Xavier Roussel, who was to marry his sister; Maurice Denis, whose interest in art profoundly influenced him; and Lugné-Poë, who was to become one of the most dynamic actor-managers of the Paris theatre of the '90s and who came to serve as an enthusiastic liaison between the writer and painter symbolists of his day.

Roussel, whom he met in 1884, was Vuillard's closest friend and it was he who seems to have influenced him most and got him to study at the Ecole des Beaux Arts, beginning in 1886, where Gérôme conducted one of the master classes. Growing discontented with the school and the teaching there, they joined forces in 1888 with a group of young rebel students at the Académie Julian, where Bouguereau was the chief teacher. This group, which included Maurice Denis, Sérusier, Bonnard, Ibels, Piot, Séguin, Vallotton and Ranson, banded together and early in 1889 called themselves the Nabis, a name derived from the Hebrew word for prophet. They were later joined by Maillol and the Dutch painter, Verkade. Their principal spokesmen were Sérusier and Denis.

Young Girl Seated. 1891. Brush drawing, 7⅛ x 7⅛". Collection John Rewald, New York

Vuillard seems at first to have been somewhat skeptical of all the enthusiastic theorizing indulged in by his friends. His first paintings of the years 1887-90 are more sensitive to atmosphere and texture than the academic realism of the schools. But they are still very conservative in drawing and restrained in color, by Nabi standards. His *Self Portrait with Varocquez* (p. 29) and the *Self Portrait in a Mirror* (color plate, p. 11), particularly the latter, suggest an early admiration for Degas, one that was to continue all his life and was, in fact, reciprocated by the older painter. The still lifes of these early years are usually studies of fruit, flowers and bottles (p. 30). They show a precise delicacy of perception and a sobriety of composition that remind one of Fantin-Latour, Chardin and possibly Vermeer. There are indications, too (color plate, p. 15), especially in the brushwork of some of these still lifes, that he had studied Manet and the impressionists and also Cézanne. The influence of the latter he may have acquired through his Nabi admiration for Cézanne's disciple, Gauguin. But he was at this time still a student, absorbing from a variety of sources whatever technical means he could. When asked once what had led him to become a painter, he replied: "I should like to say as Degas did: on Sundays they took us to the Louvre—my brother slid on the floors and I looked at the pictures."[1]

About 1890 Vuillard reached a crisis in his early career. In this year Bonnard occupied a small studio at 28 rue Pigalle, and Vuillard joined him there together with Maurice Denis and Lugné-Poë. He apparently could no longer deny the almost religious fervor of his friends. The symbolist movement, with which the Nabis were in sympathy, was then at its height. Mallarmé in poetry and Gauguin in painting were two of its leaders. In some ways a latter-day revival of the romantic movement of the first half of the nineteenth century, it sought to counter the documentary realism of the naturalist movement in letters, typified by the novels of Zola, and the literal translation of visual sensations by the impressionist painters. At the same time it fought the neo-classic verse techniques of the academic poets, the so-called Parnassians, and the mechanical "finish" of academic painters like Bouguereau and Gérôme. Led by Sérusier, who has been called St. Paul to Gauguin's Christ, the Nabis derived their first inspiration from the latter's school of Pont Aven. Emile Bernard, the admirer of Cézanne, was with Gauguin there and he, more than anyone in the Pont Aven circle, provided the theoretical basis for most of the master's anti-impressionist theories. In any case, Sérusier returned in 1888 from a summer in Brittany, bringing with him a cigar box lid on which he had demonstrated Gauguin's principles of flat, boldly outlined areas of color, signifying by their transformation and deformation of natural forms and colors the liberty of the individual artist to interpret nature according to his expressive needs. However much these principles of Gauguin may owe to the example of the Japanese print, which the impressionists had been responsible for bringing into fashion

1 Quoted by Claude Roger-Marx. *Opus cit.*, p. 15.

Self Portrait in a Mirror. 1888-90. Oil on canvas, 17½ x 21⅛". Collection Sam Salz, New York

at this time and which for Gauguin, with his penchant for the primitive and the exotic, must have had a double appeal, the fact remains that Gauguin by his messianic fervor was primarily responsible, through Sérusier, for the inception of the Nabi-symbolist theories. Furthermore, the large representation of his work in the *Peintres synthétistes et symbolistes* exhibition in 1889 at the Café Volpini provided the young Nabis with a wealth of demonstration of these same theories.

Vuillard's reaction to these symbolist theories, which were also called synthetist and neo-traditionist, is to be seen in his paintings of 1890-92; for example, *The Dressmakers* (p. 32), *Little Girls Walking* (color plate, p. 17), and *The Wood* (p. 31). They demonstrate his brilliant application of Gauguin's advice to Sérusier: "How does that tree look to you? Green? All right, then use green, the greenest green on your palette. And that shadow, a little bluish? Don't be afraid. Paint it as blue as you can!"[1] In the narrow range of his palette in these early pictures Vuillard also is following Gauguin's advice. According to Verkade, Gauguin "taught with Goethe that the artist first of all shows his strength in the limitation of his materials. Hence he allowed his pupils at first the use of only five or six colors—Prussian blue, madder-lake, cinnabar, chrome-yellow or cadmium, yellow ochre and white."[2] And surely Vuillard followed during these same years Maurice Denis' now famous dictum announced in 1890: "Remember that a picture—before being a battle horse, a female nude or some anecdote—is essentially a flat surface covered with colors assembled in a certain order."[3] In fact, Vuillard went Denis one better and avoided battle horses and anecdotes altogether and only rarely, and later in his career, painted a nude. In short, he took from the synthetist credo only its technical formulations on color and drawing and, unlike all the other Nabis with the exception of his friend Bonnard, avoided the anecdotal, peasant subjects inspired by Gauguin or the Pre-Raphaelite-like primitivism of Maurice Denis' religious pictures.

Like Bonnard he chose to stick to the world he knew intimately, in his case his home and his mother's workroom or, if he went outdoors, the familiar parade of people in the parks and gardens of Paris. This choice of subject matter has, in fact, a closer relation to the impressionists than to the symbolists. Vuillard may have known at this time an article by the impressionist critic Duranty, published in 1876 and republished in 1946 with a prefatory note saying that Vuillard had brought it to the publisher's attention. Duranty writes:

"There is for every observer a logic of color and of drawing which proceeds from an aspect, according to whether it is caught at some hour, some season, some place. This aspect is not expressed, this logic is not determined by placing Venetian materials

1 Maurice Denis. *Paul Sérusier. ABC de la Peinture, Sa Vie—Son Oeuvre*, Paris, Librairie Floury, 1942, p. 42.

2 Dom Willibrord Verkade. *Yesterdays of an Artist Monk*, New York, 1930, p. 68.

3 Maurice Denis. *Théories, 1890-1910*, Paris, 1912, p. 1. (Article first published in *Art et Critique*, 1890.)

against Flemish backgrounds, by making studio lights shine on old chests and vases. [Duranty here criticizes the practice of the academic painters of his day.] It is necessary to avoid, if one wishes to be truthful, mixing times and environments, hours and light sources. The velvety shadows, the golden lights of Dutch interiors come from the structure of the houses, from the small-paned, mullioned windows, from streets on steamy canals. With us the values of tones in interiors play with infinite variety, according to whether one is on the first or the fourth floor, whether the house is heavily furnished and carpeted, or whether it is sparsely furnished; thus, an atmosphere like a family air is created in each interior between the furniture and the objects that fill it. The frequency, the multiplicity and the disposition of the mirrors which ornament the apartments, the number of objects which run up against the walls—all these things have brought into our homes either a kind of mystery or a kind of light which can no longer be represented by Flemish means or harmonies, like adding Venetian formulae, nor by the combinations and arrangements that can be imagined in the best planned studio...

"The language of the empty apartment must be sufficiently clear so that one may deduce the character and the habits of those who live in it; and the street will tell by its passers-by what time of day it is, what moment of the public life is represented.

"The appearances of things and of people have a thousand ways of being unforeseen in reality. Our point of view is not always in the center of a room with its two lateral walls running toward that of the background; the lines and angles of cornices do not always meet with regularity and mathematical symmetry; one is not always free to suppress the expanding space in the foreground; it is sometimes very high, sometimes very low, losing the ceiling, picking up objects below, cutting off furniture unexpectedly. Our eye stops at the side at a certain distance from us, seems restricted by a frame, and it does not see the lateral objects that are caught in the margin of the frame.

"From within, it is through the window that we communicate with the outside; the window is still a frame which accompanies us without cease, lasting while we are in the house, and this time is considerable. The frame of the window, according to whether we are far from it or near it, whether we are seated or standing, cuts off the outside scene in the most unexpected, the most changing manner, procuring for us the eternal variety, the spontaneity which is one of the great zests of reality."[1]

Vuillard may well have been influenced by this impressionist approach to reality, but he added another dimension to his perception of it. Bonnard was closer to Duranty's conceptions. He depicts the Parisian scene with a child-like joy in the ever-changing patterns of movement along the streets and boulevards —discovering a new picturesqueness in ordinary, everyday sights. Vuillard's eye and temperament found a different meaning in the common things about him. Having explored to his complete satisfaction the extreme possibilities of the redness of red, the greenness of green, the blueness of blue, and having "assembled" his colors in a striking variety of orders, retaining to the full the flatness of his panel or canvas, he proceeded to explore as early as 1893, in what one feels is a Mallarméan spirit, the mysterious possibilities of an infinite gradation of color hues to extract thereby the subtlest overtones, the essential perfume of intimate objects and activities in and about his home. The progressive toning down of his earlier juxtapositions of bright areas of color to an almost

1 Edmond Duranty. *La Nouvelle Peinture. A propos du Groupe d'Artistes qui expose dans les Galeries Durand-Ruel.* (1876) New Edition, with foreword and notes by Marcel Guérin, Librairie Floury, Paris, 1946, pp. 44-46.

13

Mallarmé. c. 1896. Drawing. Private collection, Paris

whispered chorus of low notes in a minor key reminds one of the lines from a poem of Verlaine's, quoted by Huysmans in *A Rebours:*

Car nous voulons la nuance encore
Pas la couleur, rien que la nuance

. . . .

Et tous le reste est littérature.[1]

Mallarmé, speaking of the Parnassians, the academic poets of his time, said that they "take the thing just as it is and put it before us—and consequently they are deficient in mystery: they deprive the mind of the delicious joy of believing that it is creating. To name an object is to do away with the three quarters of the enjoyment of the poem which is derived from the satisfaction of guessing little by little: to suggest it, to evoke it—that is what charms the imagination."[2]

Vuillard was very familiar with these ideas of Mallarmé. He attended the famous Tuesday evenings in the poet's apartment on the rue de Rome.[3] He was sufficiently intimate with him to have painted his house at Valvins at least four

1 "For what we still desire is the nuance/Not the color, nothing but the nuance/And all the rest is literature."
2 Quoted by Edmund Wilson. *Axel's Castle,* Charles Scribner's Sons, New York, 1931, p. 20.
3 To these Tuesday evenings there also came, at one time or another, Whistler, Degas, Huysmans, Paul Valéry, André Gide, Oscar Wilde, Remy de Gourmont, Arthur Symons, George Moore and W. B. Yeats. How many of these artists and writers Vuillard met is not certain. We do know he admired Degas and knew André Gide.

Bottle with Flowers. (La Bouteille avec des fleurs.) 1889-90. Oil on canvas, 12½ x 15¾″. Collection Mr. and Mrs. Donald S. Stralem, New York

times (p. 53); and that their respect for each other was considerable is indicated by the fact that Mallarmé seriously considered having Vuillard illustrate his major dramatic poem, *Hérodiade*.

The secret charm of so many of Vuillard's small panels of the '90s is the result of his never quite "naming" an object, as Mallarmé puts it. He "suggests" it, he "evokes" it, by knitting it into an amazingly complex tapestry. And by a process of telescoping planes in a picture, for example the *Interior at l'Etang la Ville*, Roussel's home (p. 48), or *Mother and Baby* (color plate, p. 49), the foreground, middleground and background overlap and fuse into a pulsating space that bears a kind of relation to the fusion of imagery in a poem by Mallarmé.

As with all the symbolists, Vuillard and Mallarmé insist upon the primacy of art over nature. And significantly, in order to emphasize and clarify the process of symbolic transformation of nature, Mallarmé (and here he is followed by Vuillard) chooses the simplest, most intimate objects in his room, a curtain, a vase or a lamp, and by an infinitely subtle fusion of allusive conceits "charms the imagination" into an almost occult state of detachment from the object, an object that had served only as a barely referred to point of departure.

Une dentelle s'abolit	A lace curtain stands effaced
Dans le doute du Jeu suprême	In doubt of the supreme game
A n'entr'ouvrir comme un blasphème	Unfolding like a blasphemy
Qu'absence éternelle de lit.	On eternal bedlessness.
Cette unanime blanc conflit	This unanimous white conflict
D'une guirlande avec la même,	Of a garland with its like
Enfue contre la vitre blême	Vanishing on the pallid glass
Flotte plus qu'il n'ensevelit.	Is floating more than burying.
Mais chez qui du rêve se dore	But with him where dreams are gilt
Tristement dort une mandore	Sadly sleeps a mandola
Au creux néant musicien	Whose hollow void is musical
Telle que vers quelque fenêtre	Such that towards some window pane
Selon nul ventre que le sien,	According to no womb but its,
Filial on aurait pu naître.	Filial one might be born.[1]

Vuillard's fusion of images is by no means as complex or, one might say, as strained as Mallarmé's. Nor is there in his little panels the depths of melancholy of the older poet. But there is in such pictures as the *Green Lamp* (p. 57), *The Room under the Eaves* (color plate, p. 45) and *Mystery* (p. 57) a haunting note of sadness, a mysterious gloom that is truly Mallarméan. And the very compactness of these pictures, their smallness, packed to the edges as they are with suggestive imagery, recall Mallarmé's compressed, highly concentrated short

1 Mallarmé. *Poems*, translated by Roger Fry, New Directions, New York, 1951, pp. 118-119.

Little Girls Walking. 1891. Oil on canvas, 32 x 25 ⅝″. Collection Mr. and Mrs. Walter Ross, New York

poems. Above all, there is a Mallarméan narcissism in Vuillard's constant pre-occupation not only with himself in his self portraits but, by extension, with his mother—reading, preparing meals, at work as a dressmaker, engaging in all the endless little activities of a bourgeois housewife. It is as if he sees in her and in the beloved furnishings and patterned walls of his home a constant reminder, a projection of his whole being. This is the mystery, this is the secret of Vuillard, as narcissism in varying degrees is the secret of all his fellow symbolists.

If, however, Mallarmé is the dominant poetic influence on Vuillard, the pervasive influence of Redon, whom Mallarmé admired and who, after Gauguin's departure for Tahiti, became the hero of the Nabis, must not be forgotten. Not that the strange, hallucinatory content of Redon's lithographs and etchings can be remotely connected with Vuillard's interiors on the rue du Marché-Saint-Honoré. Rather, as with Mallarmé, the symbolic implications of Redon's imagery and, technically, his mastery of infinitely subtle values in his prints and later in his pastels, appealed to the idealistic Nabis as a whole and to Vuillard in particular. Furthermore, Vuillard besides being a painter was, like Bonnard and Lautrec, a printmaker of great skill and tonal delicacy. And Redon was the acknowledged master of his craft, at least to Vuillard and his friends. Their respect for him as an artist was signalized by the predominantly Nabi exhibition organized by the critic André Mellerio at Durand-Ruel's gallery

Figure in a Room. c. 1891. Watercolor, 9½ x 5½″. Collection Mr. and Mrs. H. Lawrence Herring, New York

in 1899, when Redon was given the place of honor on the walls. And when Maurice Denis came to paint his *Hommage à Cézanne* in 1900, Redon was once again included among the Nabi brethren.

By contrast, the hothouse decadence of Gustave Moreau, the teacher of Rouault and Matisse, however much his paintings may have appealed to literary symbolists like Huysmans, seems to have been antipathetic to the Nabis as a group. There are many facets to the symbolist movement, but the Nabis did not find all of them congenial to their tastes. The Baudelaire-Edgar Allen Poe strain of decadence which had its effect upon Huysmans, Verlaine and Mallarmé was too perverse and too obsessed with evil to appeal to devout young Nabis like Denis and Vuillard. And Sérusier, however far his studies led him into Semitic literature (hence, probably, the Hebrew name Nabi for his friends), theosophy and the occult, never showed any inclination in his paintings to follow anyone other than Gauguin. The overtones of Baudelairean satanism in Mallarmé were perhaps too refined to have more than an unconscious influence upon his young admirers. In Vuillard's case it is hard to find more than melancholy echoes of this particular symbolist tradition. No matter how much the imagery of Mallarmé may have appealed to him or influenced him, or how much of Baudelaire he had read, there is no conscious expression of evil in his intimate little interiors.

It is at first sight a paradox that Vuillard, who so consistently painted small, tightly organized panels, often pieces of millboard no bigger than the cigar box lid brought back by Sérusier from Pont Aven, should at the same time have painted so many large decorative panels for the homes of his friends and patrons, among them Alexandre Natanson, one of the editors of the *Revue Blanche*, the novelist Claude Anet, and Dr. Vaquez. The paradox resolves itself, however, when we recall that one of the principal tenets of the Nabi credo, derived from Gauguin, was that all art is decoration. Albert Aurier, the young critic who was the Nabis' chief spokesman, at the conclusion of an article on Gauguin, insisted that a work of art should be: "... *decorative:* for decorative painting, properly speaking, as the Egyptians and probably the Greeks and the Primitives conceived it, is nothing but a manifestation of art at once subjective, synthetist, symbolist and ideist ... Painting can only have been created to decorate with thoughts, dreams and ideas the blank walls of human buildings. The easel picture is nothing but an illogical refinement invented to satisfy the fancy or the commercial spirit of decadent civilizations." And he concluded by complaining that the world had confined Gauguin to easel pictures, and had given him no walls, not even a hovel, to paint.[1]

Verkade, the Dutch painter who became a Nabi, tells us: "In the early part of 1890 the war cry went up from studio to studio: 'No more easel pictures! Away with useless bits of furniture! Painting must not usurp a freedom which cuts it off from the other arts! The painter's work begins where the architect

1 G. Albert Aurier. "Le Symbolisme en peinture," *Mercure de France*, March, 1891.

decides that his work is finished! Give us walls and more walls to decorate! Down with perspective! The wall must be kept as a surface, and must not be pierced by the representation of distant horizons. There are no such things as pictures, there is only decoration.' "[1]

Gauguin, whose ideas and example had fired an Aurier and a Verkade to these cries for wall decorations, had in his room at Pouldu in Brittany photographs of Manet's *Olympia*, Botticelli's *Birth of Venus*, an *Annunciation* by Fra Angelico, prints of the Japanese, Utamaro, and paintings of Puvis de Chavannes. It was from such diverse sources that the Nabis and, above all, Vuillard drew their inspiration for large decorative panels. And in Vuillard's case it is not hard to see, in the first series of panels done for Alexandre Natanson in 1894, how much he owes to Puvis and to Botticelli for his decorative scheme. One has but to compare Puvis' *Sacred Grove* in the Hemicycle of the Sorbonne and Botticelli's *Spring* with *Under the Trees* (color plate, p. 34). Vuillard has drawn from both his tree-defined intervals of space, the arabesque of figure and branch set off against the verticals of tree trunks, and the blocking out of the horizon by cutting the composition off at top and sides across the thickset mass of foliage. Each of these spatial devices Vuillard uses to achieve an all-over flatness of effect in order not to destroy or penetrate the wall he is decorating. And for the same reason, whether he paints in oil on canvas or distemper on millboard, his object, like Puvis' and like the Japanese print, or the flower decorated wallpaper that was the fashion in the '90s, is to achieve a juxtaposition of flat areas of mat colors which will deploy themselves evenly over a two-dimensional wall surface.

In some of Vuillard's panels, particularly his garden scenes, one other important influence is very marked—the early paintings of Claude Monet. *The Woman in the Garden* of 1867, now in the Louvre, is the direct ancestor of *The Park* (color plate, p. 37) and the *Woman Seated in a Garden* (p. 67). Monet's pattern of striped and spotted costumes, the elegant arabesques described by figures, skirts and foliage, the dappling of sunlight and shadow as a decorative device, the framing of the picture by the cutting of the trees at top and sides— all find a flattened, airless echo in Vuillard's paintings.

The sources of Vuillard's decorative style may be many, but the finished picture is his own. Actually, by his particular selection of decorative devices—his closed, hermetic compositions, his use of arabesque motifs, the all-over pattern of his designs—he made a notable contribution to a style that sprang into fashion in the '90s, *art nouveau*. We have too long thought of *art nouveau* as a style of ornament applied to furniture, objets d'art, architecture and book illustration. Insufficient attention has been given to the Nabis' emphasis upon wall decoration and the coalescence and interdependence of their ideas with those deriving from William Morris and the English Pre-Raphaelites and the Belgian *art*

1 Quoted by Daniel-Henry Kahnweiler, *Juan Gris, His Life and Work*, translated by Douglas Cooper, Curt Valentin, New York, 1947, pp. 67-68.

Lilacs. 1892. Oil on board, 14 x 11⅛″. Collection Mr. and Mrs. Donald S. Stralem, New York

nouveau exponents, Van de Velde and Horta.[1] When the totality of Vuillard's decorative work of the '90s is properly appreciated, he may well be considered, in addition to his symbolist contribution, one of the outstanding *art nouveau* painters of his time.

In one thing Vuillard does not deviate in his decorative panels from his small paintings—the intimacy of his subject matter. His park scenes have a curious quality of the indoors about them, so enclosed and sheltered are the spaces he describes, so lacking in movement or drama are the incidents he observes— figures among the trees, almost as static as the trees themselves, a nursemaid with her charges, a woman reading in a garden, or simply sitting in a garden, figures in a room, and around a piano. Here he presents the quiet, ordinary relationships of the animate and the inanimate, the fusion of person and thing until both become one, and every shape, every color, every accent merges into a sustained tapestry-like rhythm comparable to the continuum of sound in a passage of Wagner or Debussy.[2]

André Gide, in his review of the 1905 *Salon d'Automne*, where Vuillard's masterpieces of decoration, the Vaquez panels (pp. 64, 65), were first publicly shown, said: "I do not know what I like most here. Perhaps, M. Vuillard himself. I know few works where one is brought more directly into communion with the painter. This is due, I suspect, to his emotion never losing its hold on the brush and to the outside world always remaining for him a pretext and handy means of expression. It is due to his speaking in a low tone, suitable to confidences, and to one's leaning over to listen to him . . . His melancholy is not romantic nor haughty, it is discreet and clothed in an everyday garment; it is caressingly tender, I might even say, timid, if this word were in consonance with such mastership. Yes, I see in him, his success notwithstanding, the charm of anxiety and doubt. He never puts forward a colour without excusing it by some subtle and precious withdrawal. Too modest to assert, he insinuates . . . No seeking for the showy, a constant search for harmony. By a grasp of relations, at once intuitive and studied, he explains each colour by its neighbor and obtains from both a reciprocal response . . . "[3]

When the cry first went up from the Nabi studios for walls to paint, one of the first responses seems to have come from Lugné-Poë, the actor-manager of the *Théâtre Libre* and the *Théâtre de l'Oeuvre* and an intimate friend of Vuillard, Bonnard and Maurice Denis. Lugné offered the young artists walls—the artificial walls of the stage—and all three designed and painted sets, for him and for Paul Fort's *Théâtre de l'Art*, with great enthusiasm. Unfortunately, these sets have long since been destroyed, and we can only imagine what, for example, Vuillard

1 In this connection it should be remembered that Tiffany showed stained glass windows at the *Salon* of 1895 after designs by Vuillard and other members of the Nabi group.

2 Both composers were admired by the Nabis. Wagner was indeed idolized by all the symbolists.

3 André Gide. "Promenade au Salon d'Automne," *Gazette des Beaux-Arts*, Dec. 1905, quoted from Claude Roger-Marx. *Opus cit.*, pp. 125-26.

designed for Ibsen's *Rosmersholm*, presented at the *Théâtre de l'Oeuvre* in 1893. Bonnard and another Nabi artist, Ranson, helped in the work. All we know is that Lugné-Poë said: "It was the scenery of the second act which stamped the note of intimacy and distinction on our set. Vuillard surpassed himself in ingenuity and economic invention in creating atmosphere and scenic decoration."[1] Vuillard with other Nabi artists also made lithographic designs for theatre programs, for example, one for Ibsen's *An Enemy of the People*, presented in 1893, and another for Maurice Beaubourg's *La Vie Muette*, in 1894 (p. 93). The most important theatre decorations by Vuillard, which are still happily in existence, were done not as stage sets but as decorations for the foyer of the *Comédie des Champs-Elysées*. While these were painted in 1913, long after Vuillard's first association with the theatre, they are the only major evidence we have of his devotion to the stage. The two largest panels illustrate scenes from Molière's *Le Malade Imaginaire* and Tristan Bernard's light comedy, *Le Petit Café* (p. 87). Brilliant as these panels are in the rendering of the atmosphere and lighting of the stage, the one extraordinary thing lacking in them is a sense of movement. It is as if Vuillard in both plays had been hypnotized by the scene rather than by the action and, following his own predilection for decoration, he froze the gestures of his actors in mid-air. The result is a curiously static performance—tableaux, without movement or words.

We have said that Vuillard's success was immediate in the '90s. A year older than Matisse and three years older than Rouault, he reached artistic maturity at least ten years before either of them. Like his admirer Toulouse-Lautrec, who was only four years his senior, his art reached an extraordinary degree of sophistication before he was thirty. He and his friend Bonnard, unlike so many of their fellow Nabis, "arrived" a bare four or five years after leaving art school. Both painters, like Lautrec again, are striking examples of the precociousness that was a characteristic of their *fin-de-siècle* period. And, surely because both preferred to paint rather than to theorize, they were able to apply the theories of their Nabi friends while the latter were still expounding them and worshipping at the shrine of Gauguin.

After 1900 the Nabis practically disbanded as a group. It is perhaps not fortuitous that their breakup almost coincided with the deaths of two of their heroes in 1898—Mallarmé and Puvis de Chavannes. The one represented their chief contact with the advanced literary figures of the day. Puvis, in his position as president of the Salon of the Société des Beaux-Arts, must have provided, by association, a certain cachet to the work and theories of the Nabi avant-garde. However that may be, after the dissolution, each of the Nabi brethren went his own way and, almost without exception, it was a way that ran counter to all the major movements of twentieth-century art. Sérusier, a too-devoted

---

1 Quoted by Claude Roger-Marx. *Opus cit.*, p. 18.

follower and imitator of Gauguin, was never quite able to divorce himself from the master's influence. As the years passed, his theories of painting became more abstruse and he became hopelessly involved in a numerological system of picture construction. Denis continued to write better than he painted and, no matter how increasingly devout he became, his decorative and religious paintings are but a weak expression of the intensity of his beliefs. And so with all the other Nabis except Bonnard. Verkade became a monk, and Roussel lost himself in a remote, repetitious version of Mallarmé's world of *L'Après-Midi d'un Faune*. Vallotton, whose early paintings of the '90s show something of the verve and subtlety of observation of Vuillard and Bonnard, became a stiff, tortured realist, reflecting in labored tightness of line and hard, metallic paint surface his puritan Swiss origins.

Inevitably, then, from the late careers of so many of the Nabis one gets a general feeling of frustration. Their idealistic, decorative program was so completely at odds with the temper and changing ideologies of the new century that all but one of them, Bonnard, found himself more or less stranded on the sidelines. Even Vuillard, perhaps the most brilliant of the Nabis, could not quite escape the fate of his friends.

One becomes conscious of a change in his work at the turn of the century. It is very gradual at first and is closely associated with a change about the same time in his social life. From the poetic tensions that so mark the Mallarméan years, 1893 to about 1900, he moves into a more relaxed, ostensibly less melancholy mood. His pictures reflect his new connections with a fashionable world as opposed to the old life of café discussions, literary inspiration and the close, germinal atmosphere of his own private existence at home. He now had an official dealer connection, the Bernheim brothers, and through an associate of theirs he was introduced to what must have appeared to him at first as a rather superficial company of friends, many of them, presumably, and intentionally, prospective clients. He was encouraged to paint "intimate" portraits of them, seated as casually as may be in their elaborately furnished rooms. These new interiors, larger, more elegant than those of his own home, seem to have demanded at once an increase in the scale of his panels or canvases. The old world of his own rooms and those of his sister, Mme Roussel, because they were so intimately known, so long-studied, could be compressed into a compass no bigger than ten by twelve inches. And by their very compression the intensity of their mysterious quality of intimacy was tremendously heightened. On the contrary, when he came to paint the interior of a client's house, one of his newfound fashionable friends, he found himself bound to relax his gifts of concentration, and in relaxing he enlarged his pictures accordingly.

The reduced tension is often charming. His looser brushwork and more obvious color arrangements often result in a delightful, even gay, picture which is far removed from the exquisite, brooding harmonies of many of his earlier, small panels. His decorative panels also are more loosely organized, more frankly decorative in the ordinary sense of the word. The impressionist, one

Mother and Sister of the Artist. c. 1893. Oil on canvas, 18¼ x 22¼". The Museum of Modern Art, New York. Gift of Mrs. Sadie A. May

feels, has triumphed over the symbolist. Intimacy—the close observation and transformation of a restricted, hermetic view of things—has given place to a picturesque display of technical virtuosity.

The expansion of Vuillard's social contacts, which is so closely related to his larger pictures, his more fashionable interiors, is responsible too for his now leaving Paris during the summers and spending them with his new friends in Normandy and Brittany. The result is a vacation-like enjoyment of landscape and an attempt to record his impressions of the country and the sea. Probably again because he could never quite adjust his intimate genius to unknown territory, these views of fields and harbor scenes are often conventional and unexciting. The landscape beyond his favorite Square Vintimille and the parks of Paris are too foreign, it seems, too remote from his urban-provincial world to yield to his genius for compression and distillation. From the windows of his studio it is another story (p. 84). Here the roofs and streets of his district are as familiar, as well loved, as his favorite chair.

And when he returns from the salons of his friends to his mother seated at a window (color plate, p. 90), his ability to transform and transcend the ordinary by the alchemy of his affectionate spirit is immediately evident. Perhaps his affection for older women, like that for his mother, is responsible for the relative success of such a portrait as that of Mme Bénard (p. 89), whatever its pictorial failings may be in the somewhat insensitive overconcentration on meticulously rendered detail. So too when he turns from the overstuffed luxuriousness of upper middle-class rooms to subject matter completely removed from any "society" connotations, a doctor operating (p. 88), a dentist in his office (p. 89), or his artist friends at work or in their studios (p. 91), he is able for a moment to apply his eye and hand without reservations or artistic compromise. He comes to such scenes with a Degas-like perception of the unconventional pose or incident. However unintimate some of these scenes may be, in terms of his usual milieu, the fact that they were not commissions to record the ostentatious furnishings and persons of social clients must have acted as a spur to his imagination.

Nevertheless, when all is said by way of extenuation, and however one may try to select later work that reflects something of Vuillard's original genius, the fact remains that the progress of his art during the last twenty-five years of his life, until his death in 1940, appears to us now as retrogressive, if not reactionary. Despite his extraordinary craftsmanship as a painter, as he grew older and withdrew more and more into himself, he seems to have taken an almost perverse pleasure in denying his symbolist instincts—his wonderful ability to transform and synthesize the phenomena of natural appearances—and, in an excruciating effort to record the most minute detail, he came to sacrifice, more often than not, unity in his compositions and harmony in his color orchestrations.

His defeat, such as it was, is traceable to his vulnerability to an insensitive, materialist element in Parisian society that may be said to have exploited his talents. Undoubtedly, this society, whose values were vulgarized, corrupted an artist like Vuillard who chose to serve it. The choice, however, was Vuillard's and he cannot escape the final responsibility. It is true, as a few late pictures bear witness, that he struggled to retain something of his original intimacy of feeling. But, one feels, these occasional examples of an earlier privacy of expression are in the nature of nostalgic memories of a world long past. The economic and social upheavals of the present century must have frightened him as much as they did his fashionable friends. And, for much the same reasons that they were afraid of change, he must have looked with discomfort, not to say fear, at the tensions set up by the avant-garde art movements of our time. The fauve painters, for example, who were the sensation of the 1905 *Salon d'Automne,* however decorative their intentions, were too lusty, too enthusiastic admirers of van Gogh, to suit his symbolist inheritance. The cubist revolt derived from an appreciation of Cézanne's formal discoveries that seems to have been beyond the comprehension of Vuillard and the Nabis, however much they admired the older master as an anti-impressionist pioneer. And the surrealists, with their conscious exploration of the unconscious, must have offended Vuillard's sense of privacy, if nothing else.

One concludes that the quietist, intimate genius of Vuillard was too foreign to the spirit of these times, whether social or artistic, to have waged anything but a losing battle with forces that were apparently beyond his control. Nevertheless, the extraordinary quality and maturity of his early work can never be denied and it may well have a peculiar relevance for us today. Is there possibly some connection between the striving of a Vuillard to retain something of that inwardness, that self-searching narcissism which was the symbolist's answer in the '80s and '90s to the materialism of the impressionists and the academies, and the struggle of artists today to maintain their artistic integrity at all costs? "We have lived," as Churchill has said, "through half a century of the most terrible events which have ever ravaged the human race."[1] As disillusionment has followed these tragic events, the individual has been forced in on himself in an attempt to discover some personal standards on which to base his conduct. The sensitive artist has likewise felt compelled to formulate, or express himself through, an increasingly personal imagery. Vuillard's private world of images, derived from the objects and persons intimately associated with him, may take on a new meaning, then, in the light of present-day artists' needs and desires. And in the same way that symbolist poets like Verlaine and Mallarmé have had a profound influence on twentieth-century poets, it is possible that the symbolist values of Vuillard's "intimate" paintings still have a potential significance for painters today.

1 Speech at Margate, England, October 10, 1953.

Symphony in Red. 1893. Oil on board, 23 x 25¾″. Collection Mr. and Mrs. Ralph F. Colin, New York

Vuillard and his Friend Varoquez. 1888-90. Oil on canvas, 36 x 28″. Collection Alex Lewyt, New York

Still Life. 1889-90. Oil on canvas, 18 x 25½″. Collection Mr. and Mrs. Nate B. Spingold, New York

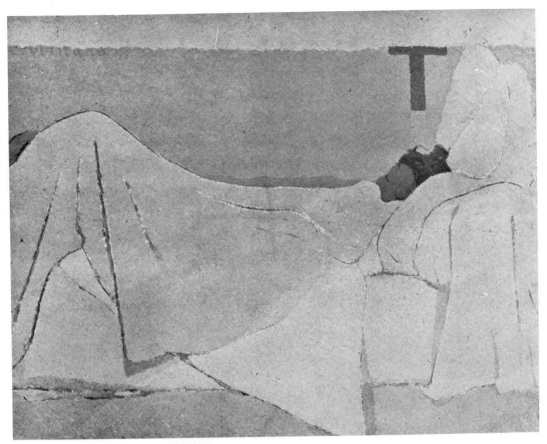

In Bed. 1891. Oil on canvas, 29⅛ x 36¼". Musée National d'Art Moderne, Paris

The Wood. c. 1892. Oil on board,
6⅝ x 9⅛". Collection Alex
Lewyt, New York

The Dressmakers. 1891. Oil on canvas, 18¾ x 21⅝″. Collection Mr. and Mrs. Ira Haupt, New York

The Flowered Dress. 1891. Oil on canvas, 14 ⅞ x 18". Private collection, New York

Under the Trees. 1894. Distemper on canvas, 84½ x 38½″. The Cleveland Museum of Art. Gift of Hanna Fund

Promenade. 1894. Distemper on canvas, 84½ x 38½″. Robert Lee Blaffer Memorial Collection, Museum of Fine Arts of Houston, Texas

The Family after the Meal. c. 1892. Oil on board, 13¼ x 19¾″. Collection Richard A. Peto, Esq., Isle of Wight, England

The Park. 1894. Distemper on canvas, 83 x 62¾″. Collection Mr. and Mrs. William B. Jaffe, New York

The Dressmaker. 1892. Oil on canvas, 9½ x 13½″. Collection Stephen C. Clark, New York

Two Women by Lamplight. 1892. Oil on canvas, 12½ x 15¾″. Musée de l'Annonciade à Saint-Tropez, France

Theatre Aisle with Toulouse-Lautrec. c. 1892. Oil on canvas, 10½ x 8¼". Collection Professor and Mrs. Raphael Salem, Cambridge, Mass.

Self Portrait in a Straw Hat. c. 1892. Oil on canvas, 14¼ x 11″. Collection Mr. and Mrs. Ralph F. Colin, New York

Railroad Station. 1892. Oil on canvas, 16 x 13″. Collection Mr. and Mrs. David Rockefeller, New York

Portrait of the Artist's Mother. c. 1897. Oil on board, 14⅛ x 11½". Collection Mr. and Mrs. William B. Jaffe, New York

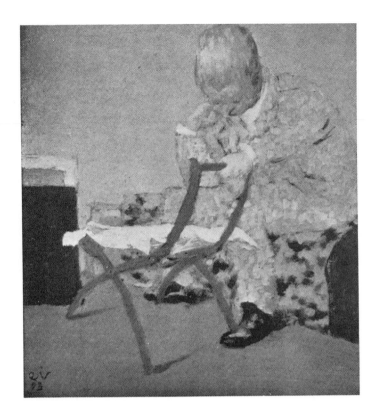

Reading. 1893. Oil on board, 11 x 11″.
Collection Philip L. Goodwin, New York

Woman in Blue. 1893. Oil on canvas, 10¼ x
8¾″. Wildenstein & Co., Inc., New York

Vuillard Family at Lunch. 1896. Oil on canvas, 12½ x 18″. Collection Mr. and Mrs. Ralph F. Colin, New York

Conversation. c. 1893. Oil on paper, 19¾ x 24¾″. Art Gallery of Toronto, Canada

44

Room under the Eaves. 1897. Oil on board, 18 x 25¾". Jacques Seligmann & Co., Inc., New York

45

Breakfast. 1893. Oil on board, 10 x 14″. Collection Mr. and Mrs. Leigh B. Block, Chicago

Woman with a Bowl. c. 1897. Oil on board, 23¼ x 21¼". Collection André Meyer, New York

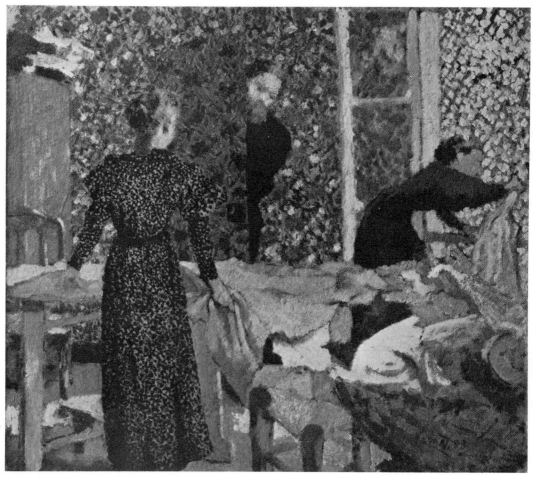

Interior at l'Etang la Ville. 1893. Oil on board, 12½ x 14⅜″. Smith College Museum of Art, Northampton, Mass.

Mother and Baby. c. 1899. Oil on board, 20 x 23″. Glasgow Art Gallery, Scotland

Woman Sweeping in a Room. c. 1892-93. Oil on board, 18 x 19″. The Phillips Gallery, Washington, D.C.

Missia and Thadée Natanson. c. 1897. Oil on canvas, 41 x 28″. Collection Mr. and Mrs. Nate B. Spingold, New York

Portrait of the Artist's Grandmother. 1894. Oil on canvas, 25 x 21″. Collection Mr. and
Mrs. Gustave Ring, Washington, D. C.

The Bench. 1895. Oil on board, 14¾ x 21½″. Collection Georges Renand, Paris

Mallarmé's House at Valvins. 1895. Oil on board, 7¼ x 15¾″. Collection Jacques Laroche, Paris

Woman Sewing. 1895. Oil on board, 12¾ x 14¾″. Museum of Fine Arts, Boston

Mother and Child. c. 1900. Oil on board, 20⅛ x 19¼″. Collection William Goetz, Los Angeles

Interior with Cipa Godebski and Missia. c. 1895. Oil on board, 24 x 20″. Collection Sir Alexander Korda, London

Mystery. c.1895. Oil on board,
14⅛ x 15⅛″. Carstairs Gallery, New York

The Green Lamp. c. 1895. Oil on board, 14 x 27¼″. Collection Richard A. Peto, Esq., Isle of Wight, England

57

Family at Table. c. 1897. Oil on board, 19 x 27″. Collection Mr. and Mrs. Fernand Leval, New York

Café Scene. c. 1895. Oil on board, 12 x 11″. Collection Leonard C. Hanna, Jr., Cleveland, Ohio

The Luncheon. 1897. Oil on board, 12⅝ x 21¾″. Paul Rosenberg & Co., New York

The Art Talk. 1898. Distemper on board, 10¾ x 15¾″. Collection Mr. and Mrs. Leon A. Mnuchin, New York

The Ferryman. 1897. Oil on board, 20½ x 29½″. Musée National d'Art Moderne, Paris

Woman Seated in a Room. 1899. Oil on canvas, 28 x 27″. Hillman Periodicals, Inc., New York

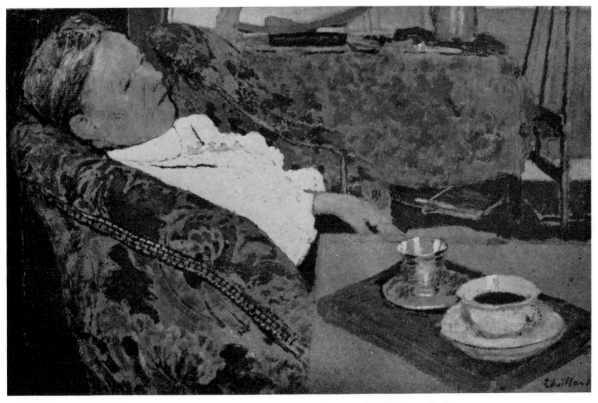

Artist's Mother Resting. c. 1897. Oil on board, 14 x 22''. Estate of Millicent A. Rogers

The Reader (Vaquez decoration). 1896. Distemper on canvas, 82 x 60″. Musée du Petit Palais, Paris. (Not in the exhibition)

The Piano (Vaquez decoration). 1896. Distemper on canvas, 82 x 60″. Musée du Petit Palais, Paris. (Not in the exhibition)

Woman Reading in a Garden. 1898. Distemper on canvas, 84½ x 63⅜". Collection James Dugdale, Esq., of Crathorne, England

Woman Seated in a Garden. 1898. Distemper on canvas, 84½ x 63⅜″. Collection James Dugdale, Esq., of Crathorne, England

Alfred Natanson and his Wife. 1900. Oil on paper, 21¼ x 26½". Collection Mr. and Mrs. Nate B. Spingold, New York

The Newspaper. c. 1898. Oil on board, 13½ x 21½″. The Phillips Gallery, Washington, D. C.

Conversation (Cipa and Missia Godebski). 1899. Oil on board, 15½ x 19¾″. Collection Mr. and Mrs. Jacques Gelman, Mexico City

The Natanson Brothers, Missia, and Léon Blum. c. 1898-1900. Oil on board, 17 x 20″.
Collection Diane Esmond Wallis, New York

Self Portrait. 1903. Oil on board, 16⅛ x 13⅛". Collection Mr. and Mrs. Donald S. Stralem, New York

Above: *The Meal*. c. 1899. Oil on canvas, 27½ x 28″. Collection Henry P. McIlhenny, Philadelphia

Mother in Profile. c. 1898. Oil on canvas, 13 x 14⅞″. Collection Mr. and Mrs. John Hay Whitney, New York

Child in a Room. c. 1900. Oil on board, 17⅛ x 23¾". The Art Institute of Chicago

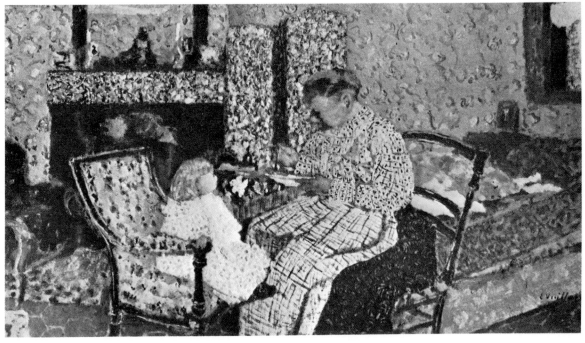

Annette's Lunch. 1901. Oil on board, 13½ x 24″. Musée de l'Annonciade à Saint-Tropez, France

The Painter Ker-Xavier Roussel and his Daughter. c. 1902. Oil on board, 22½ x 20½″. Room of Contemporary Art, Albright Art Gallery, Buffalo, N. Y.

Portrait of the Painter Roussel. 1898. Oil on board, 25½ x 17″. Collection
Mr. and Mrs. Ralph F. Colin, New York

Near Criquebeuf. 1905. Oil on board, 17¾ x 23¾″. Collection Richard S. Zeisler, New York

View from the Artist's Studio. c. 1906. Oil on canvas, 16¾ x 13½″. Collection Sam Salz, New York

View in Switzerland. 1900. Oil on board, 16 x 32¼". Private collection, New York

View from the Artist's Studio, rue de la Pompe. c. 1905. Oil on canvas, 28 x 62″. Collection Mr. and Mrs. Harry Lynde Bradley, Milwaukee

The Chaise Longue. c. 1900. Distemper on board, 23¾ x 24⅞″. Collection Mr. and Mrs. Richard Rodgers, New York

Girl with a Doll. 1906. Oil on canvas, 19 x 23¾″. Collection Mr. and Mrs. Leo Glass, New York

Le Square Vintimille. 1908-1917. Distemper on canvas, 63½ x 90″. Collection Mrs. Daniel Wildenstein, New York

The Art Dealers. 1908. Oil on canvas, 28⅞ x 26″. Collection Mr. and Mrs. Richard K. Weil, St. Louis

Interior. 1903. Distemper on board, 31½ x 37½″. Collection Mr. and Mrs. Morris Sprayregen, New York

Scene from Molière's "Le Malade Imaginaire." 1913. Distemper on canvas, 71 x 118″. Decoration for the foyer of the *Comédie des Champs-Elysées*, Paris

Scene from Tristan Bernard's "Le Petit Café." 1913. Distemper on canvas, 71 x 110¼″. Decoration for the foyer of the *Comédie des Champs-Elysées*, Paris

Dr. Gosset Operating. 1912, 1936. Distemper on canvas, 64 x 91''. Private collection, France

Dr. Louis Viau in his Office. 1937. Distemper on board, 36¼ x 33″. Private collection, Corsica

Madame Bénard. c. 1930. Distemper on canvas, 44⅛ x 39⅜″. Musée National d'Art Moderne, Paris

The Window. c. 1914. Distemper on board, 32⅝ x 21¼″. Collection Alex Lewyt, New York

Study for Portrait of Pierre Bonnard. 1925. Distemper on paper, 45 x 56¼".
Musée du Petit Palais, Paris

Study for Portrait of Maurice Denis. 1925. Distemper on paper, 44 x 54".
Musée du Petit Palais, Paris

Notes on Vuillard as a Printmaker

One of the many minor factors which loosely gathered the Nabi painters as a group was their common interest in printmaking. Their chief mentor, after Gauguin's escape to Tahiti, became Odilon Redon, an active lithographer since 1879. Toulouse-Lautrec, another friend, had already initiated his famous series of lithographs. The renaissance of lithography in France had even captured a popular audience. Poster designers such as Chéret and Toulouse-Lautrec had wrested the medium from the domination of commercial printers, and their bold inventions could be seen everywhere on the walls and kiosks of Paris. It seems only natural that in the 1890's many of the Nabis, among them Bonnard, Denis, Roussel and Vuillard, should have begun to work on stone. By 1895 they had found in the dealer Ambroise Vollard an editor who was eager to commission and publish their lithographs. Of the Nabis only Vallotton concentrated on the woodcut.

Artists such as Denis and Vallotton were unable to carry into the twentieth century the brilliance of their earlier style as painters or their former production as printmakers. It is interesting that the majority of Vuillard's prints also belong to the decade of the 1890's.

In the winter of 1892-93 Vuillard began the study of lithography in the studio of the master printer Ancourt where both Toulouse-Lautrec and Bonnard were accustomed to work. During the next four years he drew about thirty subjects mostly in black and white but occasionally in two or three colors. Lithographs printed in black such as *Interior* (p. 93) and *Intimacy*, whose very titles might characterize Vuillard's art, are much more successful than any of his first experiments in color. And often, sometimes by scratching into the stone itself, he achieved an airy delicacy never equalled by Bonnard in black and white.

Many of Vuillard's smaller lithographs were published by the magazine the *Revue Blanche* or issued as programs for theatrical productions of *L'Oeuvre* (p. 94). Four of Vuillard's programs are for plays by Ibsen and, among other playwrights, appear Strindberg and Hauptmann. These programs for *L'Oeuvre* were usually so composed that Vuillard had space on the same stone to draw an advertisement for the *Revue Blanche*.

Vuillard received his first commission from Ambroise Vollard in 1896, the color lithograph *The Garden of the Tuileries*, issued in an album of twenty-two prints by as many artists. To a similar publication the following year, Vuillard contributed *Children Playing* (p. 94) and, for Vollard's next collection, printed but unfortunately never published, another color lithograph as well as the cover of the album itself.

In his lithographs for Vollard, Vuillard worked exclusively in color. Tech-

Interior with Screen. c. 1893. Lithograph, 9 ⅞ x 12 ⅛''. The Museum of Modern Art, New York

nically they are often extremely complex, and Vuillard usually employed five or six different stones for the various colors necessary for each print. He was helped by Auguste Clot, the printer most responsible for the success of Vollard's publications.

In February 1899 Vollard exhibited an album of thirteen color lithographs entitled *Paysages et Intérieurs* (pp. 95, 100). This series, his most important work as a printmaker, can be compared only with Bonnard's album *Quelques Aspects de la Vie de Paris,* which had been Vollard's debut as a publisher in 1895. In Vuillard's album, as in several of his other prints, the vivid realization of the out of doors comes as a surprise in relation to his work as a painter.

It was not Vollard but the German scholar and editor Meier-Graefe who commissioned Vuillard's most ambitious lithograph. In 1901 Meier-Graefe published *Germinal,* an imposing album of large-scale prints and reproductions. One of the stellar contributions was Vuillard's *The Garden outside the Studio,* more than two by one and one-half feet, printed in eight colors. Lithographs by Vuillard were also included in two other German albums of fine prints, *Pan* and *Insel,* as well as in *L'Oeuvre* and *L'Estampe Originale,* published in Paris.

During the 1890's Vuillard had drawn fifty lithographs, half of which were in color. During the twentieth century he drew less than a dozen, all in black and white. The most curious is a study of Cézanne after a self portrait. Six of the later lithographs belong to *Cuisine,* a collection of recipes printed in 1935 to which de Segonzac and de Villeboeuf each contributed six etchings.

Vuillard's first intaglio print was a portrait of the Belgian painter van Rysselberghe etched around 1898. His other etchings consist of two studies of women, done in 1924 and 1930, and, in 1937, four views of the Square Vintimille

La Vie Muette (program for l'Oeuvre). 1894.
Lithograph, 12¼ x 9½". The Museum of Modern
Art, New York

Children's Game. 1897. Color lithograph, 10¼ x 17⅝". The Museum of Modern
Art, New York

94

Interior with Pink Wallpaper I and II. 1899. Two color lithographs, 14 x 11″ each. The Museum of Modern Art, New York. Gift of Mrs. John D. Rockefeller, Jr.

opposite his apartment at the foot of Montmartre. Five of Vuillard's seven etchings, gathered posthumously in 1944, were printed as illustrations for Jean Giraudoux's *Le Tombeau de Edouard Vuillard.*

Before the turn of the century many of the best young French painters had been intrigued by the possibilities of the poster as a form of visual communication. Vuillard, however, attempted only one *affiche*—an advertisement of about 1894 for a beverage whose slogan capitalized on the new vogue for cycling as well as the new taste for apéritifs: "Bicyclists take BECANE—an appetizing liqueur, a reconstructing tonic with a meat base."

Unlike Bonnard, Vuillard did not consistently continue to make prints after 1900. Nor was he attracted to book illustration, although in 1898 Vollard had proposed Mallarmé's *Hérodiade.* Mallarmé wrote to Vollard: "I am glad to know that I am being published, mon cher, by a picture dealer. Don't let Vuillard leave Paris without having given you a favorable reply. To encourage him, say that I am pleased with the length of the poem."

Although limited in quantity and restricted in period, a few of Vuillard's single prints are landmarks in the history of modern printmaking. And in color lithography nothing has ever excelled the brilliance and freshness of his album *Paysages et Intérieurs.*

WILLIAM S. LIEBERMAN

Chronology

1868 Born, November 11, Cuiseaux, Saône-et-Loire. Youngest of family of three. Father a retired colonial army officer. Mother, Marie Michaud, daughter of textile designer and manufacturer. Vuillard's uncle Sorel made designs for cashmere shawls.

1877 Family moves to Paris.

1883 Father dies. Mother sets herself up in business as a dressmaker with two helpers. Workroom in apartment on the rue Daunou, later on ground floor of home on the rue du Marché-Saint-Honoré.

1884 Vuillard meets Roussel, a fellow student at the Lycée Condorcet. Maurice Denis was also a fellow student there, as was Lugné-Poë, who was to become a leading theatre director. Mallarmé taught English in this same lycée, leaving in this year to teach at the Lycée Janson.

1886 At Roussel's instigation begins art studies at the Ecole des Beaux-Arts where Gérôme was the principal teacher.

1888 Changes, with Roussel, to the Académie Julian to join forces with Maurice Denis, Bonnard, Ibels, Vallotton, Ranson and Sérusier. Bouguereau was the chief master at this school. Sérusier returns from visiting Gauguin to expound the latter's synthetist theories.

1889 All these young painters band together under the name of Nabis—a name derived from the Hebrew word for prophet. Gauguin's paintings in the *Peintres symbolistes et synthetistes* exhibition at the Café Volpini of great influence on them.

1890 Vuillard, Bonnard, Denis and Lugné-Poë share a studio at 28 rue Pigalle. Vuillard designs a program for Lugné-Poë's *Théâtre Libre*. Denis publishes the first article of his "Théories" in *Art et Critique*.

1891 Begins exhibiting with the other Nabis at Le Barc de Boutteville's. Also exhibits in the offices of the *Revue Blanche* (founded in this year by the Natanson brothers). At these exhibitions he and his friends were "discovered" by the critics Gustave Geffroy, Arsène Alexandre, Roger Marx and Albert Aurier. Aurier's article *Le Symbolisme en Peinture* published in the March issue of *Mercure de France*. About this time Vuillard begins to attend the famous Tuesday evenings at the home of Mallarmé.

1892 First decorative paintings: six panels and screen for Mme Desmarais, now lost. First comes in contact with the art dealer Jos. Hessel, who was associated with the Bernheim brothers. Hessel, through Vuillard's regard for his wife, increasingly influences Vuillard's career. Exhibition of the Nabis at Le Barc de Boutteville's. Albert Aurier's review appears in article, "Les Symbolistes," in the *Revue Encyclopédique*, 1892, pp. 474-86. Aurier calls Vuillard an "intimiste Verlainien."

1893 Vuillard, Roussel, Bonnard and Ranson work together on the scenery for Ibsen's *Rosmersholm* at Lugné-Poë's new *Théâtre de l'Oeuvre*. Previously the Nabis had collaborated in work for Paul Fort's *Théâtre de l'Art* and the *Théâtre des Marionettes*. Unfortunately all these sets, including those for *Rosmersholm*, have been destroyed. Roussel marries Vuillard's sister, Marie.

1894 Commissioned by Alexandre Natanson, one of the editors of the *Revue Blanche*, to decorate his home. For this purpose Vuillard produces a series of nine large panels representing a synthesis of scenes from the public parks of Paris.

1895 Tiffany shows a series of stained glass windows at the Salon, one designed by Vuillard.

1896 Invited with Lautrec and Bonnard to exhibit with *La Libre Esthétique* in Brussels. Paints four large panels, now in the Petit Palais, for his friend Dr. Vaquez, to decorate the latter's drawing room in his house on the Boulevard Haussmann. Moves from the rue du Marché-Saint-Honoré to the rue Truffaut in the Batignolles quarter.

1898 Decorations for the novelist Claude Anet. The two most important panels of this series passed into the hands of Princesse Antoine Bibesco and are now the property of James Dugdale, Esq., of Crathorne.

1899 Vollard publishes Vuillard's series of lithographs, *Paysages et Intérieurs*. The Nabis show for the last time together as a group at Durand-Ruel's.

1903- Exhibits with Bernheim-Jeune, irregularly at the
1914 *Salon des Indépendants*, and more consistently at the *Salon d'Automne* (until 1911), of which he was one of the founders. Spends his summers in Brittany and Normandy with the Hessels and their friends.

1904 Moves from the rue Truffaut to the rue de la Tour, near the Trocadero.

1908 Paints a series of decorative panels, representing views of Paris, for Henri Bernstein. Moves from the rue de la Tour to the rue de Calais, near the Place Vintimille. Later moves to a house on the Square Vintimille.

1913 Decorations for the foyer of the *Comédie des Champs Elysées*. Visits London and Holland with Bonnard.

1914 Mobilized into the territorial army to serve as a home guard.

1928 Death of his mother.

1930 Visits Spain with Prince Bibesco.

1936 Forty small pictures included in *Peintres de la Revue Blanche*, an exhibition in connection with the celebration of the fiftieth anniversary of symbolism at the Bibliotèque Nationale.

1937 Decoration for the Palais de Chaillot, entitled *Comedy*.

1938 Elected to the *Institut*. Large retrospective exhibition at the Musée des Arts Décoratifs, the selection supervised by himself. Decoration for the Palace of the League of Nations at Geneva; the subject, *Peace Protecting the Muses*.

1940 In poor health, he is persuaded to leave Paris ahead of the German advance, but dies shortly afterwards at La Baule, June 21.

Bibliography

The following is a selection of references favoring items accessible in local collections. Material now in this library is marked *. With a few exceptions, exhibition catalogs and similar texts noted in the standard periodical indexes have been omitted. Since almost all significant citations on Vuillard are contained in the bibliographies specified, no detailed inventory is required for the purpose of the present catalog.

Bernard Karpel, Librarian of the Museum

*1 ARTES (Antwerp). [Vuillard number]. No. 2, 1946. *November issue; articles by C. Roger-Marx, E. Langui; catalog of exhibition at the Fransch-Belgische Kultureel Akkord.*

2 AURIER, G.-ALBERT. Oeuvres posthumes. Paris, Mercure de France, 1893.

*3 BAZIN, GERMAIN. L'Époque impressioniste. 104 p. Paris, Tisné, 1953. *First edition 1947. Bibliography on impressionism, neo-impressionism and symbolism.*

4 BAZIN, GERMAIN. Lautrec raconté par Vuillard. *L'Amour de l'Art* 12 no.4:141-142 Apr 1931. *English summary.*

4a BENDER. Maurice Denis. *In* Thieme, U. & Becker, F. Allgemeines Lexikon der bildenden Künstler. v.9, p.69-71 Leipzig, Seemann, 1913. *Bibliography.*

*5 BENET, RAFAEL. Simbolismo. 203 p. plus 272 illus. Barcelona, Omega, 1953. *Bibliography.*

*6 BERNE. KUNSTHALLE. Die Maler der Revue Blanche: Toulouse-Lautrec und die Nabis. [34]p. 1951. *Exhibition catalog; bibliography.*

*7 BERNHEIM-JEUNE, J. & G., COLLECTION. L'Art moderne. v.2, p.83-86 Paris, Bernheim-Jeune, 1919. *Early critiques by Mirbeau, Fagus, Natanson, Hepp.*

*8 BRUSSELS. PALAIS DES BEAUX-ARTS. Vuillard (1868-1940); préface de Claude Roger-Marx. 32 p. Bruxelles, La Connaissance, 1946.

*9 CHASSÉ, CHARLES. Le Mouvement symboliste dans l'Art du XIXᵉ Siècle. 215 p. Paris, Floury, 1947.

*10 CHASTEL, ANDRÉ. E. Vuillard. *Art News* 52 no. 7 pt. II: 35-57, 180-185 (passim) Nov 1 1953. *Art News Annual no. 23 (1954). Illustrations p.27-34, 39-42, 51, 54.*

*11 CHASTEL, ANDRÉ. Vuillard, 1868-1940. 123 p. Paris, Floury, 1946. *Chronology, list of exhibitions, bibliography.*

*12 COGNIAT, RAYMOND. Décors de Théâtre. [50]p. plus plates Paris, Chroniques du Jour, 1930. *Lists scenic work by Vuillard.*

*13 COOLUS, ROMAIN. Edouard Vuillard. *L'Art Vivant* no. 221:23-36 May 1938.

*14 COQUIOT, GUSTAVE. Cubistes, Futuristes, Passéistes. p. 200-203 Paris, Ollendorf, 1914. *Another edition 1923.*

15 DENIS, MAURICE. L'époque du symbolisme. *Gazette des Beaux-Arts* 76 no. 854: 165-179 Mar 1934.

*16 DENIS, MAURICE. Théories 1890-1910: Du Symbolisme et de Gauguin vers un nouvel Ordre classique. 4. éd. Paris, Rouart & Watelin, 1920. *First edition, 1912; supplemented by "Nouvelles Théories" (1922).*

*17 DORIVAL, BERNARD. Les Étapes de la Peinture française contemporaine. v.1, p.103-180 Paris, Gallimard, 1943. *Bibliography.*

*18 ESCHOLIER, RAYMOND. La Peinture française, XXᵉ Siècle. p.8-26 Paris, Floury, 1937.

*19 FELS, FLORENT. L'Art Vivant de 1900 à nos Jours. p.136-140 Genève, Cailler, 1950.

*20 FOSCA, FRANÇOIS. Edouard Vuillard. *L'Amour de l'Art* 1:127 1920.

*21 GAUTHIER, E. P. Lithographs of the Revue Blanche, 1893-1895. *Magazine of Art* 45:273-278 Oct 1952.

22 GEFFROY, GUSTAVE. Histoire de l'Impressionisme: La Vie artistique. v.2, p.378-382 Paris, Floury, 1893.

*23 GEORGE, WALDEMAR. Vuillard et l'âge heureux. *L'Art Vivant* no.221: 26-36 May 1938.

23a GIDE, ANDRÉ. Promenade au salon d'automne. *Gazette des Beaux-Arts* no.582:479-481 Dec 1905.

*24 GIRAUDOUX, JEAN. Tombeau de Edouard Vuillard. Orné de 5 Gravures originales à l'eau-forte. Pour les Amis de Vuillard. [26]p. including plates [1944].

*25 GOLDWATER, ROBERT. Symbolist art and theater. *Magazine of Art* 39:366-370 Dec 1946.

*26 GROHMANN, WILL. Edouard Vuillard. *In* Thieme, U. & Becker, F. Allgemeines Lexikon der bildenden Künstler. v.34, p.585-586 Leipzig, Seemann, 1940. *Extensive bibliography.*

*27 HESS, WALTER. Die Farbe in der modernen Malerei. p.74-87 München, Universität München, 1950. *On Denis and Sérusier. Unpublished typescript; bibliography.*

*28 HUMBERT, AGNÈS. Le Groupe de Nabis. *Art-Documents* (Genève) no. 31:8-9, 13 Apr 1953; no.34: 15 July 1953; no.37: 1 Oct 1953.

*29 HUYGHE, RENÉ, ed. Histoire de l'Art contemporain: la Peinture. p. 69-96 illus Paris, Alcan, 1935. *"Les Nabis" by Bazin, Chassé, Dupont, Fegdal, Huyghe, Sterling. Biographical and bibliographical notes. Previously published in L'Amour de l'Art, no.4, Apr 1933.*

*30 JOHNSON, UNA E. Ambroise Vollard, Editeur. p.158-162 New York, Wittenborn, 1944.

30a LAROCHE, HENRY-JEAN. Cuisine, Recueil de 117 Recettes. Paris, Arts et Métiers Graphiques, 1935. *Includes 6 lithographs by Vuillard.*

31 LECLÉRE, TRISTAN. Edouard Vuillard. *Art et Décoration* 37:97-106 illus Oct 1920.

32 LUGNÉ-POË, ALEXANDRE. La Parade. 2 vol. Paris, Nouvelle Revue française, 1930-32.

33 MARGUÉRY, HENRI. Les Lithographies de Vuillard. [32]p. Paris, L'Amateur d'Estampes, 1935. *Previously published in L'Amateur d'Estampes no.5-6 Oct-Dec 1934.*

*34 MEIER-GRAEFE, JULIUS. *Entwicklungsgeschichte der modernen Kunst.* v.1, p.171-175 Stuttgart, Hoffmann, 1904. *Second edition, 1927.*

*35 MELLERIO, ANDRÉ. La Lithographie originale en Couleurs. p.7, 11, 14, 28, 30 Paris, L'Estampe et L'Affiche, 1898.

*36 MELLERIO, ANDRÉ. Le Mouvement idéaliste en Peinture. 72 p. Paris, Floury, 1896.

*37 MELLOT, DENISE, ed. Vuillard dans ses lettres. *Arts* no. 160:8 illus Apr 2 1948.

*38 MERCANTON, JACQUES. Vuillard, et le Goût de Bonheur. 10 p. plus 10 col. plates Paris, Skira, 1949.

*39 NATANSON, THADÉE. Peints à leur Tour. p.364-383 Paris, Michel, 1948.

40 NATANSON, THADÉE. Un groupe de peintres. *La Revue Blanche* v.5 Nov 1893. *Additional references: Apr. 15, 1898; May 1 1900; May 1 1901.*

*41 NATANSON, THADÉE. Sur Edouard Vuillard. *Arts et Métiers Graphiques* no. 65:38-40 Nov 1938.

*42 NATANSON, THADÉE. Sur une exposition des peintres de la Revue Blanche. *Arts et Métiers Graphiques* no. 54:9-18 Aug 15 1936.

*43 PARIS. MUSÉE DES ARTS DÉCORATIFS. Exposition E. Vuillard, mai-juillet. 56 p. illus 1938.

44 PUVIS DE CHAVANNES, HENRI. Un entretien avec Vuillard sur Puvis. *La Renaissance* 9 no.2:87-90 Feb 1926.

*45 RAYNAL, MAURICE. Modern Painting, p. 38-39, 322-323 et passim Geneva & New York, Skira, 1953.

46 REWALD, JOHN. Extraits du journal inédit de Paul Signac. *Gazette des Beaux-Arts* 36:97-128 July-Sept. 1949; 39:265-284 Apr 1952. *English summary.*

*47 ROGER-MARX, CLAUDE. Edouard Vuillard. *Le Portique* no.3:47-55 1946.

48 ROGER-MARX, CLAUDE. Edouard Vuillard, 1867-1940. *Gazette des Beaux-Arts* 29:263-277 June 1946.

49 ROGER-MARX, CLAUDE. Edouard Vuillard à l'Institut. *La Renaissance* 21:67-69 Mar 1938. *English Summary, p.74. Also see Bulletin de l'Institut for Vuillard's "Les envois des pensionnaires de l'Académie de France à Rome en 1938" and "en 1939."*

*50 ROGER-MARX, CLAUDE. Les premières époques de Vuillard. *Art et Industrie* no.2:67-70 Feb 1946.

*51 ROGER-MARX, CLAUDE. L'Oeuvre gravé de Vuillard. [182]p. including plates [Paris &] Monte Carlo, Sauret, 1948.

*52 ROGER-MARX, CLAUDE. Vuillard: his Life and Work. 211 p. New York, La Maison Française and London, P. Elek, 1946. *Bibliography, p. 209-210. Translation of French edition: Paris, Arts et Métiers Graphiques, 1945. Another monograph (76 p.) issued 1948.*

*53 SALOMON, JACQUES. Auprès de Vuillard. 120 p. Paris, La Palme, 1953.

*54 SALOMON, JACQUES. Vuillard: Témoignage de Jacques Salomon. 151 p. Paris, Michel, 1945. *"Notes," p.143-146.*

*55 SAN LAZZARO, G. di. Painting in Paris, 1895-1949. p.26-37 New York, Philosophical Library, 1949. *Italian edition: Roma, Danesi, 1945.*

56 SEGARD, ACHILLE. Peintres d'Aujourd'hui—les Décorateurs. v.2, p.247-303, 320-322 Paris, Ollendorf, 1914.

*57 SÉRUSIER, PAUL. ABC de la Peinture, suivi d'une Étude sur la Vie et l'Oeuvre de Paul Sérusier par Maurice Denis. 123 p. Paris, Floury, 1942. *First edition 1921. Another edition issued 1950, with correspondence collected by Mme Sérusier.*

*58 STRECKER, PAUL. Edouard Vuillard. *Das Kunstwerk* 6 no. 3:19-20 1952. *Followed page 21-23 by "Paul Sérusier und die Schule von Pont Aven" (H. Troendle).*

59 VEBER, PIERRE. Mon ami Vuillard. *Nouvelles Littéraires* no.811:6 Apr 30 1938.

*60 VENTURI, LIONELLO. Impressionists and Symbolists. 244 p. New York, London, Scribner, 1950.

61 VERKADE, Dom WILLIBRORD. Yesterdays of an Artist-Monk. London, Burns, Oates & Washbourne, New York, Kenedy, 1930. *Translated from the German. Best edition: Le Tourment de Dieu: Étapes d'un Moine Peintre (Paris, Rouart & Watelin, 1923).*

*62 VUILLARD, EDOUARD. Cahier de Dessins. Notice de Jacques Salomon; préface de Annette Vaillant. [16]p. plus 50 plates Paris, Quatre Chemins, 1950.

63 VUILLARD, EDOUARD. Paysages et Intérieurs [Douze lithographies en couleurs]. Paris, Vollard, 1899. *Also cover.*

*64 VUILLARD, EDOUARD. Peintures, 1890-1930. Introduction de André Chastel. 7p. plus 16 col. plates Paris, Editions du Chêne, 1948.

*65 WILD, DORIS. Der "intimist" Vuillard als monumental Maler. *Werk* 34 no.12:400-404 Dec 1947. *Also her: Moderne Malerei. p.119-121 Konstanz, Europa, 1950.*

*66 WILDENSTEIN GALLERY, LONDON. Edouard Vuillard. 17 p. 1948. *June exhibit; text by C. Roger-Marx.*

*67 WILENSKI, R. H. Modern French Painters. 424 p. New York, Harcourt, Brace, 1949.

*68 WRIGHT, WILLARD H. Modern Painting. p.164-206 New York & London, Lane, 1915.

Catalog of the Exhibition

Lenders to the Exhibition

Alphonse Bellier, Paris; Mr. and Mrs. Leigh B. Block, Chicago; Mr. and Mrs. Harry Lynde Bradley, Milwaukee; Mr. and Mrs. Sidney F. Brody, Los Angeles; Mr. and Mrs. Albert K. Chapman, Rochester, N. Y.; Stephen C. Clark, New York; Mr. and Mrs. Ralph F. Colin, New York; Mme D. David-Weill, Paris; Gaston T. de Havenon, New York; Peter H. Deitsch, New York; James Dugdale, Esq., of Crathorne, England; Mr. and Mrs. James W. Fosburgh, New York; Mr. and Mrs. Jacques Gelman, Mexico City; Mrs. Charles Gilman, New York; Mr. and Mrs. Leo Glass, New York; William Goetz, Los Angeles; Philip L. Goodwin, New York; Leonard C. Hanna, Jr., Cleveland; Mr. and Mrs. Ira Haupt, New York; Mr. and Mrs. H. Lawrence Herring, New York; Hillman Periodicals, Inc., New York; Mr. and Mrs. William B. Jaffe, New York; Marcel Kapferer, Paris; Sir Alexander Korda, London; Jacques Laroche, Paris; Mr. and Mrs. Fernand Leval, New York; Alex Lewyt, New York; Henry P. McIlhenny, Philadelphia; André Meyer, New York; Mrs. Gerrish Milliken, New York; Mr. and Mrs. Leon A. Mnuchin, New York; Richard A. Peto, Esq., Isle of Wight, England; Georges Renand, Paris; John Rewald, New York; Mr. and Mrs. Gustave Ring, Washington, D. C.; Mr. and Mrs. David Rockefeller, New York; Nelson A. Rockefeller, New York; Mr. and Mrs. Richard Rodgers, New York; Estate of Millicent A. Rogers; Mrs. Nettie Rosenstein, New York; Mr. and Mrs. Walter Ross, New York; Professor and Mrs. Raphael Salem, Cambridge, Mass.; Jacques Salomon, Paris; Mr. and Mrs. Nate B. Spingold, New York; Mr. and Mrs. Morris Sprayregen, New York; Mr. and Mrs. Donald S. Stralem, New York; Diane Esmond Wallis, New York; Mr. and Mrs. Richard K. Weil, St. Louis; Mr. and Mrs. John Hay Whitney, New York; Mrs. Daniel Wildenstein, New York; Richard S. Zeisler, New York.

Albright Art Gallery, Buffalo; The Art Gallery of Toronto; The Art Institute of Chicago; The Cleveland Museum of Art; Glasgow Art Gallery, Scotland; Kunstmuseum, Winterthur, Switzerland; Musée de l'Annonciade à Saint-Tropez, France; Musée National d'Art Moderne, Paris; Musée du Petit Palais, Paris; Museum of Fine Arts, Boston; The Museum of Fine Arts of Houston; The Museum of Modern Art, New York; The Phillips Gallery, Washington, D. C.; Smith College Museum of Art, Northampton, Mass.; Le Théâtre et la Comédie des Champs-Elysées, Paris.

Carstairs Gallery, New York; Fine Arts Associates, New York; Paul Rosenberg & Co., New York; Sam Salz, New York; Jacques Seligmann & Co., New York; Weyhe Gallery, New York; Wildenstein & Co., Inc., New York.

Catalog

The Cleveland Museum of Art: January 26-March 14, 1954

The Museum of Modern Art, New York: April 7-June 6, 1954

In dimensions height precedes width. Items marked with an asterisk are illustrated.

In the designation of media, distemper is used as the English equivalent of the French, détrempe: *colors mixed with glue.*

Self Portrait in a Mirror. 1888-90. Signed. Oil on canvas, 17½ x 21⅛". Lent by Sam Salz, New York. *Color plate p. 11*

Vuillard and His Friend Varocquez. 1888-90. Oil on canvas, 36 x 28". Lent by Alex Lewyt, New York. *Ill. p. 29*

Self Portrait. 1888-90. Oil on canvas, 15¾ x 12¼". Lent by Jacques Salomon, Paris

Still Life. c. 1889. Signed. Oil on canvas, 8¼ x 12¼". Lent by Jacques Salomon, Paris

Bottle with Flowers. (La Bouteille avec des fleurs.) 1889-90. Signed. Oil on canvas, 12½ x 15¾". Lent by Mr. and Mrs. Donald S. Stralem, New York. *Color plate p. 15*

Still Life. 1889-90. Signed. Oil on canvas, 18 x 25½". Lent by Mr. and Mrs. Nate B. Spingold, New York. *Ill. p. 30*

Still Life with Apple. c. 1890. Signed. Oil on canvas, 13 x 16¼". Lent by Mr. and Mrs. Ralph F. Colin, New York

In Bed. 1891. Signed and dated. Oil on canvas, 29⅛ x 36¼". Lent by the Musée National d'Art Moderne, Paris. *Ill. p. 31.* New York only

The Dressmakers. 1891. Signed. Oil on canvas, 18¾ x 21⅝". Lent by Mr. and Mrs. Ira Haupt, New York. *Ill. p. 32*

The Flowered Dress. 1891. Signed and dated. Oil on canvas, 14⅞ x 18". Lent anonymously. *Ill. p. 33*

Woman at the Door. 1891. Signed and dated. Oil on board, 11½ x 8". Lent by Mr. and Mrs. Donald S. Stralem, New York

Little Girls Walking. 1891. Signed. Oil on canvas, 32 x 25⅝". Lent by Mr. and Mrs. Walter Ross, New York. *Color plate p. 17*

Young Girl Seated. 1891. Signed. Brush drawing, 7⅞ x 7⅛". Lent by John Rewald, New York. *Ill. p. 9*

Figure in a Room. c. 1891. Signed. Watercolor, 9½ x 5½". Lent by Mr. and Mrs. H. Lawrence Herring, New York. *Ill. p. 18*

Two Women by Lamplight. 1892. Signed and dated. Oil on canvas, 12½ x 15¾". Lent by the Musée de l'Annonciade à Saint-Tropez, France. *Ill. p. 38*

The Artist's Mother. 1892. Signed and dated. Wash drawing, 10 x 7½". Lent by John Rewald, New York

Lilacs. 1892. Signed. Oil on board, 14 x 11⅛". Lent by Mr. and Mrs. Donald S. Stralem, New York. *Color plate p. 21*

Railroad Station. 1892. Signed. Oil on canvas, 16 x 13". Lent by Mr. and Mrs. David Rockefeller, New York. *Ill. p. 40*

Mother in the Kitchen. 1892. Signed. Oil on canvas, 13 x 10". Lent by Sam Salz, New York

Self Portrait. 1892. Oil on board, 14⅛ x 11". Lent by Jacques Salomon, Paris

The Dressmaker. 1892. Signed. Oil on canvas, 9½ x 13½". Lent by Stephen C. Clark, New York. *Ill. p. 38*

Self Portrait. 1892. Signed. Oil on board, 14 x 11". Lent by Mr. and Mrs. Sidney F. Brody, Los Angeles. *Color frontispiece.* New York only

"Au Divan Japonais." Profile of Yvette Guilbert. 1892. Oil on board, 8 x 8". Lent by Diane Esmond Wallis, New York. New York only

The Wood. c. 1892. Signed. Oil on board, 6⅝ x 9⅛". Lent by Alex Lewyt, New York. *Ill. p. 31*

Self Portrait in a Straw Hat. c. 1892. Signed. Oil on canvas, 14¼ x 11". Lent by Mr. and Mrs. Ralph F. Colin, New York. *Ill. p. 40*

Breakfast. c. 1892. Signed. Oil on board, 12¾ x 8⅝". Lent by Mr. and Mrs. William B. Jaffe, New York

Family after the Meal. c. 1892. Signed. Oil on board, 13¼ x 19¾". Lent by Richard A. Peto, Esq., Isle of Wight, England. *Ill. p. 36*

Theatre Aisle with Toulouse-Lautrec. c. 1892. Oil on canvas, 10½ x 8¼". Lent by Professor and Mrs. Raphael Salem, Cambridge, Mass. *Ill. p. 39*

Woman Sweeping in a Room. c. 1892-93. Signed. Oil on board, 18 x 19". Lent by The Phillips Gallery, Washington, D. C. *Ill. p. 50*

Interior at l'Etang la Ville. 1893. Signed and dated. Oil on board, 12½ x 14⅜". Lent by the Smith College Museum of Art, Northampton, Mass. *Ill. p. 48*

Interior at l'Etang la Ville. 1893. Signed and dated. Oil on canvas, 13 x 16". Lent by Stephen C. Clark, New York

Woman in Blue. 1893. Signed and dated. Oil on canvas, 10¼ x 8¾". Lent by Wildenstein & Co., Inc., New York. *Ill. p. 42*

Interior. 1893. Signed and dated. Oil on canvas, 18 x 15". Lent by the Kunstmuseum, Winterthur, Switzerland

Reading. 1893. Signed and dated. Oil on board, 11 x 11". Lent by Philip L. Goodwin, New York. *Ill. p. 42*

Breakfast. 1893. Signed. Oil on board, 10 x 14". Lent by Mr. and Mrs. Leigh B. Block, Chicago. *Ill. p. 46*

Symphony in Red. 1893. Signed. Oil on board, 23 x 25¾". Lent by Mr. and Mrs. Ralph F. Colin, New York. *Color plate p. 28*

Mother and Sister of the Artist. c. 1893. Signed. Oil on canvas, 18¼ x 22¼". The Museum of Modern Art, New York. Gift of Mrs. Sadie A. May. *Color plate p. 25*

The Conversation. c. 1893. Signed. Oil on paper, 19¾ x 24¾". Lent by The Art Gallery of Toronto, Canada. *Ill. p. 44*

Portrait of Mme Hessel. c. 1893. Signed. Oil on board, 18¾ x 13¾". Lent by Gaston T. de Havenon, New York

The Dressmaker's Shop. c. 1893. Oil on canvas, 18¼ x 45½". Lent by Mr. and Mrs. Walter Ross, New York

Under the Trees. 1894. Signed and dated. Distemper on canvas, 84½ x 38½". The Cleveland Museum of Art. Gift of Hanna Fund. *Color plate p. 34*

Promenade. 1894. Signed and dated. Distemper on canvas, 84½ x 38½". Lent from the Robert Lee Blaffer Memorial Collection, The Museum of Fine Arts of Houston, Texas. *Color plate p. 35*

The Park. 1894. Signed. Distemper on canvas, 83 x 62¾". Lent by Mr. and Mrs. William B. Jaffe, New York. *Color plate p. 37*

Portrait of the Artist's Grandmother. 1894. Signed. Oil on canvas, 25 x 21". Lent by Mr. and Mrs. Gustave Ring, Washington, D.C. *Ill. p. 52*

The Little Restaurant. c. 1894. Signed. Oil on board, 11 x 9". Lent by Georges Renand, Paris

The Bench. 1895. Signed and dated. Oil on board, 14¾ x 21½". Lent by Georges Renand, Paris. *Ill. p. 53*

Woman Sewing. 1895. Signed and dated. Oil on board, 12¾ x 14¾". Lent by the Museum of Fine Arts, Boston, Mass. *Ill. p. 54*

Mallarmé's House at Valvins. 1895. Signed and dated. Oil on board, 7¼ x 15¾". Lent by Jacques Laroche, Paris. *Ill. p. 53*

Café Scene. c. 1895. Signed. Oil on board, 12 x 11". Lent by Leonard C. Hanna, Jr., Cleveland. *Ill. p. 59*

The Green Lamp. c. 1895. Signed. Oil on board, 14 x 27¼". Lent by Richard A. Peto, Esq., Isle of Wight, England. *Ill. p. 57*

Interior with Cipa Godebski and Missia. c. 1895. Signed. Oil on board, 24 x 20″. Lent by Sir Alexander Korda, London. *Ill. p. 56*

Mystery. c. 1895. Signed. Oil on board, 14⅛ x 15⅛″. Lent by the Carstairs Gallery, New York. *Ill. p. 57*

Black Cat in Courtyard. c. 1895. Signed. Oil on board, 7⅜ x 6¾″. Lent by Mrs. Gerrish Milliken, New York

Vuillard Family at Lunch. 1896. Signed. Oil on canvas, 12½ x 18″. Lent by Mr. and Mrs. Ralph F. Colin, New York. *Color plate p. 43*

The Ferryman. 1897. Signed and dated. Oil on board, 20½ x 29½″. Lent by the Musée National d'Art Moderne, Paris. *Ill. p. 61*

Room under the Eaves. 1897. Signed and dated. Oil on board, 18 x 25¾″. Lent by Jacques Seligmann & Co., Inc., New York. *Color plate p. 45*

The Luncheon. 1897. Signed and dated. Oil on board, 12⅝ x 21¾″. Lent by Paul Rosenberg & Co., New York. *Ill. p. 60*

Missia and Thadée Natanson. c. 1897. Signed. Oil on canvas, 41 x 28″. Lent by Mr. and Mrs. Nate B. Spingold, New York. *Color plate p. 51*

The Artist's Mother Resting. c. 1897. Signed. Oil on board, 14 x 22″. Lent by the Estate of Millicent A. Rogers. *Ill. p. 63*

Family at Table. c. 1897. Signed. Oil on board, 19 x 27″. Lent by Mr. and Mrs. Fernand Leval, New York. *Color plate p. 58*

Portrait of the Artist's Mother. c. 1897. Signed. Oil on board, 14⅛ x 11½″. Lent by Mr. and Mrs. William B. Jaffe, New York. *Color plate p. 41*

Woman with a Bowl. c. 1897. Oil on board, 23¼ x 21¼″. Lent by André Meyer, New York. *Color plate p. 47.* New York only

Portrait of the Painter Roussel. 1898. Signed and dated. Oil on board, 25½ x 17″. Lent by Mr. and Mrs. Ralph F. Colin, New York. *Ill. p. 77*

Woman Reading in a Garden. 1898. Signed and dated. Distemper on canvas, 84½ x 63⅜″. Lent by James Dugdale, Esq., of Crathorne, England. *Ill. p. 66*

Woman Seated in a Garden. 1898. Signed and dated. Distemper on canvas, 84½ x 63⅜″. Lent by James Dugdale, Esq., of Crathorne, England. *Ill. p. 67*

The Art Talk. 1898. Signed. Distemper on board, 10¾ x 15¾″. Lent by Mr. and Mrs. Leon A. Mnuchin, New York. *Ill. p. 60*

Missia Natanson Sewing. 1898. Signed. Oil on board, 18 x 19″. Lent by Wildenstein & Co., Inc., New York

An Evening of Music. 1898. Signed. Oil on board, 18 x 22″. Lent by Mr. and Mrs. Donald S. Stralem, New York

Mother in Profile. c. 1898. Signed. Oil on canvas, 13 x 14⅞″. Lent by Mr. and Mrs. John Hay Whitney, New York. *Ill. p. 73*

The Newspaper. c. 1898. Signed. Oil on board, 13½ x 21½″. Lent by The Phillips Gallery, Washington, D.C. *Ill. p. 69*

The Natanson Brothers, Missia, and Léon Blum. c. 1898-1900. Oil on board, 17 x 20″. Lent by Diane Esmond Wallis, New York. *Ill. p. 71.* New York only

The Writer. 1899. Signed. Oil on canvas, 18½ x 22½″. Lent by Mr. and Mrs. Richard K. Weil, St. Louis

Conversation (Cipa and Missia Godebski). 1899. Signed. Oil on board, 15½ x 19¾″. Lent by Mr. and Mrs. Jacques Gelman, Mexico City. *Ill. p. 70*

Woman Seated in a Room. 1899. Signed. Oil on canvas, 28 x 27″. Lent by Hillman Periodicals, Inc., New York. *Color plate p. 62*

The Meal. c. 1899. Signed. Oil on canvas, 27½ x 28″. Lent by Henry P. McIlhenny, Philadelphia. *Ill. p. 73.* New York only

Mother and Baby. c. 1899. Signed. Oil on board, 20 x 23″. Lent by the Glasgow Art Gallery, Scotland. *Color plate p. 49*

Alfred Natanson and his Wife. 1900. Signed. Oil on paper, 21¼ x 26½″. Lent by Mr. and Mrs. Nate B. Spingold, New York. *Color plate p. 68*

Woman Sewing, Interior. 1900. Signed. Oil on canvas, 18 x 25½″. Lent by William Goetz, Los Angeles

View in Switzerland. 1900. Signed. Oil on board, 16 x 32¼″. Lent anonymously. *Color plate p. 80*

The Chaise Longue. c. 1900. Signed. Distemper on board, 23¾ x 24⅞″. Lent by Mr. and Mrs. Richard Rodgers, New York. *Color plate p. 82*

Mother and Child. c. 1900. Signed. Oil on board, 20⅛ x 19¼″. Lent by William Goetz, Los Angeles. *Color plate p. 55*

The Arbor. c. 1900. Signed. Distemper on canvas, 23½ x 18½″. Lent by Jacques Laroche, Paris

Mme Vuillard with a Carafe. c. 1900. Signed. Oil on board, 16¾ x 15¾″. Lent by Jacques Laroche, Paris

Child in a Room. c. 1900. Oil on board, 17⅛ x 23¾″. Lent by The Art Institute of Chicago. *Ill. p. 74*

Annette's Lunch. 1901. Signed. Oil on board, 13½ x 24″. Lent by the Musée de l'Annonciade à Saint-Tropez, France. *Ill. p. 75*

The Painter Ker-Xavier Roussel and his Daughter. c. 1902. Signed. Oil on board, 22½ x 20½″. Lent from the Room of Contemporary Art, Albright Art Gallery, Buffalo. *Ill. p. 76*

Woman Reading. 1903. Signed and dated. Oil on canvas, 23½ x 26″. Lent by Mrs. Nettie Rosenstein, New York

*Self Portrait. 1903. Signed. Oil on board, 16⅛ x 13⅛″. Lent by Mr. and Mrs. Donald S. Stralem, New York. *Color plate p. 72*

*Interior. 1903. Signed. Distemper on board, 31½ x 37½″. Lent by Mr. and Mrs. Morris Sprayregen, New York. *Color plate p. 86*

Missia at the Piano. 1904. Signed and dated. Oil on board, 20⅞ x 24″. Lent by Paul Rosenberg & Co., New York

Vase of Flowers. 1904. Signed and dated. Oil on board, 23⅝ x 22⅞″. Lent by the Musée National d'Art Moderne, Paris

At the Seashore. c. 1904. Signed. Oil on board, 8½ x 8½″. Lent by Sam Salz, New York

*Near Criquebeuf. 1905. Signed. Oil on board, 17¾ x 23¾″. Lent by Richard S. Zeisler, New York. *Ill. p. 78*

Le Café Wepler. c. 1905. Signed. Oil on canvas, 24½ x 40⅝″. The Cleveland Museum of Art. Gift of Hanna Fund

Mme Hessel Resting. c. 1905. Signed. Oil on canvas, 17 x 25½″. Lent by Mr. and Mrs. Albert K. Chapman, Rochester, New York

*View from the Artist's Studio, rue de la Pompe. c. 1905. Oil on canvas, 28 x 62″. Lent by Mr. and Mrs. Harry Lynde Bradley, Milwaukee. *Ill. p. 81*

*Girl with a Doll. 1906. Signed and dated. Oil on canvas, 19 x 23¾″. Lent by Mr. and Mrs. Leo Glass, New York. *Ill. p. 83*

*View from the Artist's Studio. c. 1906. Signed. Oil on canvas, 16¾ x 13½″. Lent by Sam Salz, New York. *Ill. p. 79*

Anemones. 1907. Signed and dated. Distemper on board, 21½ x 21″. Lent by Mr. and Mrs. Donald S. Stralem, New York

The Luncheon. 1908. Oil on board, 8½ x 16½″. Lent by Mr. and Mrs. James W. Fosburgh, New York

*The Art Dealers. 1908. Signed. Oil on canvas, 28⅞ x 26″. Lent by Mr. and Mrs. Richard K. Weil, St. Louis, through the courtesy of the City Art Museum of St. Louis. *Ill. p. 85*

*Le Square Vintimille. 1908-1917. Signed. Distemper on canvas, 63½ x 90″. Lent by Mrs. Daniel Wildenstein, New York. *Ill. p. 84. New York only*

Interior. c. 1910. Signed. Distemper on board, 45 x 22½″. Lent by the Fine Arts Associates, New York

Annette at Villerville. c. 1910. Distemper on paper, 68½ x 48¾″. Lent by Jacques Salomon, Paris

Child at Lunch. 1911. Signed. Oil on canvas. Lent anonymously

*Dr. Gosset Operating. 1912, 1936. Signed. Distemper on canvas, 64 x 91″. Lent anonymously. *Ill. p. 88*

*Scene from Tristan Bernard's "Le Petit Café." 1913. Signed and dated. Distemper on canvas, 71 x 110½″. Lent by Le Théâtre et la Comédie des Champs-Elysées, Paris. *Ill. p. 87. New York only*

*Scene from Molière's "Le Malade Imaginaire." 1913. Signed and dated. Distemper on canvas, 71 x 118″. Lent by Le Théâtre et la Comédie des Champs-Elysées, Paris. *Ill. p. 87. New York only*

Dr. Georges Viau in his Office. 1914. Signed and dated. Distemper on board, 43¼ x 55⅛″. Lent anonymously

*The Window. c. 1914. Signed. Distemper on board, 32⅝ x 21¼″. Lent by Alex Lewyt, New York. *Color plate p. 90*

Figures in an Interior. c. 1915. Signed. Distemper on board, 35½ x 31″. Lent by Mrs. Charles Gilman, New York

The Artist's Mother. c. 1917. Signed. Distemper on board, 25 x 23″. Lent by the Estate of Millicent A. Rogers

Dr. Vaquez Operating. c. 1917. Signed. Pastel on paper, 25½ x 20″. Lent by Georges Renand, Paris

Lunch (Mme Vuillard). c. 1917? Signed. Oil on board, 23 x 28¼″. Lent by Alphonse Bellier, Paris

Mme Kapferer. 1919. Signed and dated. Distemper on canvas, 50¾ x 37⅜″. Lent by Marcel Kapferer, Paris

Three drawings for *Dr. Vaquez at the Hospital*. c. 1921. Signed. Pencil on paper, No. 1. 7⅞ x 5″; No. 2. 7⅞ x 4⅞″; No. 3. 7⅞ x 4⅞″. Lent by Georges Renand, Paris

Mme Tristan Bernard in her Drawing Room. 1925. Signed and dated. Oil on canvas, 11½ x 14″. Lent by Alex Lewyt, New York

*Study for Portrait of Maurice Denis. 1925. Signed. Distemper on paper, 44 x 54″. Lent by the Musée du Petit Palais, Paris. *Ill. p. 91*

*Study for Portrait of Pierre Bonnard. 1925. Signed. Distemper on paper, 45 x 56¼″. Lent by the Musée du Petit Palais, Paris. *Ill. p. 91*

The Artist's Mother Smiling. c. 1925. Signed. Drawing, 23¾ x 29⅛″. Lent by Jacques Salomon, Paris

In the Studio. c. 1925. Signed. Pastel, 21⅝ x 19¾″. Lent by Mme D. David-Weill, Paris

The Housewife (Mme Vuillard). c. 1925. Signed. Oil on board, 16¼ x 11¼″. Lent by Jacques Laroche, Paris

Siesta. 1928? Signed and dated. Pencil and watercolor, 6¾ x 4⅜″. The Museum of Modern Art, New York. Gift of Sam Salz

Still Life. c. 1928. Signed. Pastel, 20 x 20½″. Lent by Mme D. David-Weill, Paris

*Madame Bénard. c. 1930. Signed. Distemper on canvas, 44⅛ x 39⅜″. Lent by the Musée National d'Art Moderne, Paris. *Ill. p. 89*

Study for Portrait of the Comtesse de Noailles. c. 1932. Signed. Charcoal on canvas, 43¼ x 50¼″. Lent by the Musée National d'Art Moderne, Paris

Portrait of the Comtesse de Noailles. c. 1932. Signed. Oil on canvas, 43½ x 50½″. Lent by Sam Salz, New York

*Dr. Louis Viau in his Office. 1937. Signed. Distemper on board, 36¼ x 33″. Lent anonymously. *Ill. p. 89*

Portrait of Sam Salz. 1937. Gouache and pastel, 20 x 13½″. Lent by Sam Salz, New York

Vase of Flowers. Pencil, 6⅝ x 4″. The Museum of Modern Art, New York. Gift of Sam Salz

Prints

The definitive catalog of Vuillard's prints referred to as RM is *L'Oeuvre gravé de Vuillard* by Claude Roger-Marx, see bibl. 51.

Siesta (The Convalescence). 1893. Color lithograph, 11½ x 9″. (RM 2). The Museum of Modern Art, New York. Gift of Mrs. John D. Rockefeller, Jr.

*Interior with Screen. c. 1893. Lithograph printed in black, 9⅞ x 12⅛″. (RM 8). The Museum of Modern Art, New York. *Ill. p. 93*

"Rosmersholm" (program for *L'Oeuvre*). 1893. Lithograph printed in black, 8¼ x 12¼″. (RM 16). The Museum of Modern Art, New York

*"La Vie Muette" (program for *L'Oeuvre*). 1894. Lithograph printed in black, 12¼ x 9½″. (RM 20). The Museum of Modern Art, New York. *Ill. p. 94*

"Lisez la *Revue Blanche*" and "Au dessus des forces humaines" (program for *L'Oeuvre*). 1894. Two lithographs printed in black from one stone, 12 x 18¾″. (RM 18). The Museum of Modern Art, New York

Intimacy. c. 1894. Lithograph printed in black, 10⅜ x 7⅞″. (RM 10). The Museum of Modern Art, New York

The Dressmaker. 1894. Color lithograph, 9¾ x 6⅜″. (RM 13). The Museum of Modern Art, New York

The Tuileries. 1895. Lithograph printed in green, 9½ x 10¾″. (RM 27). Lent by Nelson A. Rockefeller, New York

The Garden of the Tuileries. 1896. Color lithograph, 11⅛ x 17″. (RM 28). Lent by the Weyhe Gallery, New York

Mother and Child. 1896. Color lithograph, 7½ x 9″. (RM 30). The Museum of Modern Art, New York

*Children's Game. 1897. Color lithograph, 10¼ x 17⅝″. (RM 29). The Museum of Modern Art, New York. *Ill. p. 94*

Cover for *L'Album des Peintres-Graveurs.* 1898. Color lithograph, 23½ x 18″. (RM 47). The Museum of Modern Art, New York

From *Paysages et Intérieurs.* An album of 13 color lithographs. The Museum of Modern Art, New York. Gift of Mrs. John D. Rockefeller, Jr.

Cover. 1899. Color lithograph, 20⁹⁄₁₆ x 15⅞″. (RM 31)

The Game of Checkers. 1899. Color lithograph, 14⅜ x 11″. (RM 32)

The Avenue. 1899. Color lithograph, 12⅜ x 16⁵⁄₁₆″. (RM 33)

Across the Fields. 1899. Color lithograph, 10⅛ x 14⅜″. (RM 34)

*Interior with Pink Wallpaper I. 1899. Color lithograph, 14 x 11″. (RM 36). *Ill. p. 95*

*Interior with Pink Wallpaper II. 1899. Color lithograph, 14 x 11″. (RM 37). *Ill. p. 95*

The Hearth. 1899. Color lithograph, 14½ x 10⅞″. (RM 39)

Two Girls on the Pont de L'Europe. 1899. Color lithograph, 12⅛ x 15″. (RM 40)

Café Terrace at Night. 1899. Color lithograph, 14⅝ x 11¹⁄₁₆″. (RM 41)

The Cook. 1899. Color lithograph, 14⅛ x 10⅞″. (RM 42)

The Two Sisters-in-Law. 1899. Color lithograph, 14½ x 11½″. (RM 43)

The Birth of Annette. c. 1899. Color lithograph, 13⅜ x 15¾″. (RM 44). Lent by Peter H. Deitsch, New York

A Balcony at the Gymnasium. 1900. Color lithograph, 10 x 7⅞″. (RM 48). The Museum of Modern Art, New York

The Garden outside the Studio. 1901. Color lithograph, 24¾ x 18⅞″. (RM 45). Lent by Nelson A. Rockefeller, New York

Portrait of Cézanne. 1914. Lithograph printed in black, 9 x 9½″. (RM 51). The Museum of Modern Art, New York

Tombeau de Edouard Vuillard, a book by Jean Giraudoux (see bibl. 24). Contains 5 etchings, 1898 to 1937, printed posthumously. (RM 61, 62, 64, 65, 66). The Museum of Modern Art, New York